TAXONOMY OF EDUCATIONAL OBJECTIVES

The Classification of Educational Goals

HANDBOOK II: AFFECTIVE DOMAIN

By

David R. Krathwohl
Michigan State University

Benjamin S. Bloom
University of Chicago

Bertram B. Masia
University of Chicago

Longman
New York & London

TAXONOMY OF EDUCATIONAL OBJECTIVES
Handbook II: Affective Domain

Longman Inc., 95 Church Street, White Plains, N.Y. 10601
Associated companies, branches, and representatives throughout the world.

Fourteenth Printing by Longman Inc.

Library of Congress Cataloging in Publication Data

Main entry under title:

Taxonomy of educational objectives.

Bibliographical footnotes.
CONTENTS.—handbook 1. Cognitive domain.—handbook 2. Affective domain.
1. Education—Aims and objectives. I. Bloom, Benjamin Samuel, 1913- ed. II. Title.
LB17.T3 370.1 64-12369
ISBN: 0-582-28239-X (previously ISBN: 0-679-30210-7)

Manufactured in the United States of America

ACKNOWLEDGMENTS

The persons listed below contributed to the Taxonomy Project through attending one or more of the conferences at which the development of the affective domain was discussed.

BENJAMIN S. BLOOM
University of Chicago

PAUL S. BURNHAM
Yale University

HENRY CHAUNCEY
Educational Testing Service

RUTH CHURCHILL
Antioch College

WILLIAM COLEMAN
Coleman Associates

MARY CORCORAN
University of Minnesota

LEE J. CRONBACH
University of Illinois

HAROLD L. DAHNKE,
Michigan State University

PAUL L. DRESSEL
Michigan State University

SYDNEY DUNN
Australian Council for Educational Research

HENRY DYER
Educational Testing Service

ROBERT EBEL
Michigan State University

MAX ENGELHART
Chicago Public Schools

WARREN FINDLEY
University of Georgia

WILLIAM H. FOX*
Indiana University

EDWARD J. FURST
Ohio State University

NATHANIEL L. GAGE
Stanford University

RAYMOND J. GERBERICH
American Educational Research Association

RALPH GOLDNER
New York University

J. THOMAS HASTINGS
University of Illinois

LOUIS M. HEIL
Brooklyn College

WALKER H. HILL
Michigan State University

CLARK HORTON
Dartmouth College

DAVID R. KRATHWOHL
Michigan State University

WILBUR L. LAYTON
Iowa State University

M. RAY LOREE
University of Alabama

CHRISTINE MCGUIRE
College of Medicine, University of Illinois

JOHN V. MCQUITTY
University of Florida

LOUIS B. MAYHEW
Stanford University

*Deceased

William B. Michael
University of California,
Santa Barbara

John B. Morris
University of Mississippi

C. Robert Pace
University of California,
Los Angeles

Lynette Plumlee
Sandia Corporation

Herman H. Remmers
Purdue University

Phillip Runkel
University of Illinois

David Saunders
Princeton, New Jersey

Enoch I. Sawin
San Francisco State College

George G. Stern
Syracuse University

Wilson B. Thiede
University of Wisconsin

Ralph W. Tyler
Center for Advanced Study in the
Behavioral Sciences

Willard G. Warrington
Michigan State University

Rex Watt*
University of Southern California

---

* Deceased

PREFACE

The success of *Taxonomy of Educational Objectives, Handbook I: Cognitive Domain,* has spurred our work on the *Affective Domain*. As is indicated in the text, we found the affective domain much more difficult to structure, and we are much less satisfied with the result. Our hope is, however, that it will represent enough of an advance in the field to call attention to the problems of affective-domain terminology. Further, we hope that it will hold the affective domain's terms well enough in place to facilitate research and thinking on these problems. If it achieves these goals, revisions and modifications of the framework should be possible in the not too distant future, and we should be able at least to approach the specificity and clarity with which we can now handle phenomena in the cognitive domain. How large a step we have taken in this direction remains for you, the reader, to judge.

This *Handbook* is modeled in format after *Handbook I: Cognitive Domain.* The reader will find that Part I describes the nature of the affective domain and the classification structure prepared for it. Part II gives the classification structure in detail and describes the evaluation of affective objectives at each level of the structure. In Part I, Chapters 1 and 2 give the background of the project and indicate how and why it came to be. Chapter 3 describes the basis of classification (internalization) and the nature of the classification structure, and relates internalization to terms common to the field. Chapter 4 analyzes the relation of the affective to the cognitive domain. Chapter 5 describes how the affective-domain structure can be used to classify both objectives and test items, and it permits the reader to test himself on how well he can use the *Taxonomy*. Chapter 6 relates the affective domain to the contemporary views of curriculum, evaluation, and educational research and suggests some points for further exploration.

Part II contains a complete and detailed description of the categories and subcategories of the affective domain and gives illustrative objectives and test items for each category.

For easy reference, Appendix A contains a condensed version of the *Affective Domain.* Since the *Cognitive Domain* is frequently referred to in the text, a condensed version of it is included in Appendix B.

Readers seeking a hasty overview of the *Affective Domain* should read at least Chapters 1, 3, 5, and Appendix A.

One problem which occurred with frequency in reviews of the preliminary manuscript may be worth noting here, though it is also described in Chapter 3. The categories of the affective-domain structure are developed to handle primarily positive values rather than aversions, fears, and dislikes. This is because this is the way in which educational objectives are generally stated, and the *Taxonomy* is a framework for classifying these objectives. But evaluation procedures may measure both the positive and negative aspects. It is believed that, with very little interpretation (for example, as is shown on page 30), the framework can be used for those "negative" types of objectives which one is likely to find in the school curriculum.

The authors are most grateful for the advice and assistance they received from many sources. As is indicated in more detail in Chapter I, efforts to develop the affective framework began while the *Cognitive Domain* was being finished. Different possible structures for the domain were discussed at a number of meetings of the Association of College and University Examiners. Persons who attended these meetings and thus contributed to the development of the structure are listed on a previous page. Records of attendance at the meetings are not complete, however. We apologize for any omissions. The last of the meetings of this group occurred in 1957.

Special recognition is due to the Social Science Research Council's Committee on Personality Development in Youth for financial aid toward some of the expenses of travel, critics, and clerical services, and to Dr. C. Robert Pace of U.C.L.A., a member of the SSRC Committee, and Dr. Ralph W. Tyler, Director, Center for Advanced Study in the Behavioral Sciences, the chairman of the SSRC Committee, who encouraged the authors. We are grateful to the University of Chicago and to Michigan State University for the research time and facilities they provided.

We wish particularly to thank Dr. Warren Findley, University of Georgia, Dr. Willard Spalding, California Coordinating

Council for Higher Education, and Dr. Asahel Woodruff, University of Utah, for careful readings and detailed comments on the manuscript, and Dr. Milton Rokeach, Michigan State University, for especially helpful comments on Chapter 4.

In addition the authors received helpful written comments and suggestions from Dr. Roscoe A. Boyer, University of Mississippi; Miss Dorothy Frayer, Miami University; Dr. Edward J. Furst, Ohio State University; Mr. Louis Hofmann, Michigan State University; Dr. John U. Kidd, University of Pittsburgh; Dr. Harry Levin, Cornell University; Dr. M. Ray Loree, University of Alabama; Dr. Robert MacGregor, University of Texas; Dr. Enoch I. Sawin, San Francisco State College; and Dr. Godfrey Stevens, University of Pittsburgh.

EAST LANSING, MICHIGAN D.R.K.
CHICAGO, ILLINOIS B.S.B.
B.B.M.

CONTENTS

Part I

Introduction and Explanation

Part II

The Affective Domain Taxonomy

The Classification Scheme
Illustrative Educational Objectives
Illustrative Test Items

PART I

INTRODUCTION AND EXPLANATION

CHAPTER 1

OVERVIEW OF THE TAXONOMY PROJECT

First Work on the Taxonomy

In 1948 a group of psychologists interested in achievement testing met at an American Psychological Association Convention in Boston. After considerable discussion on the difficulties of cooperating and communicating about work on educational evaluation, it became clear to us that a special limitation of this work was the absence of a common frame of reference. We grew quite enthusiastic about the possibilities of several schemes for securing, at the minimum, a common terminology for describing and referring to the human behavioral characteristics we were attempting to appraise in our different school and college settings.

It became apparent, after further discussion, that we each began the process of test construction with a detailed set of specifications, a blueprint for the test. One part of these specifications described the content with which the test was to deal. This might be, for example, a subject matter (mathematics, history, physics), or an area of human experience (music, religion, reading, social relations), or an aspect of the self (leisure-time activities, feelings about self, etc.). There was apparently no limit to the content of our appraisals. They ranged over all the areas of human experience, subject matter included in the curriculum, and objects constructed by, used by, or thought about by, human beings. Library classifications, encyclopedia indexes, and philosophic divisions do attempt to summarize the contents and objects of human interest and inquiry. We as a group could see little advantage to be gained for our work by creating one more classification of subject matter and areas of experience.

It was the other dimension of our specifications—the types of *human reaction* or *response* to the content, subject matter, problems, or areas of human experience—which seemed most significant for our purposes. We had all made use of educational objectives, defined in terms of thoughts, feelings, and actions, as this second dimension. These embraced a range of human responses, including knowing about something, solving problems of various kinds, evincing an interest in some types of human experience, having an attitude toward some object or process, or expressing one's feelings and views on a variety of phenomena. Such objectives specify in operational terms the actions, feelings, and thoughts students are expected to develop as a result of the instructional process. It seemed to us that some way of classifying and ordering the types of responses specified as *desired outcomes* of education might be useful to a group of achievement examiners.

We believed that objectives of education might gain meaning through two rather distinct processes. One process is that of defining the objective in behavioral terms and then determining the evidence (i.e., tasks, tests, observations, etc.) which is relevant in judging whether students have or have not "achieved" the objective. This is a type of operational definition which has been an integral part of curriculum and evaluation work for the past three decades. A second process is that of trying to place an objective within a large over-all scheme or matrix. It is this second process to which the classifications in the proposed taxonomy were addressed. Here it was hoped that placing the objective within the classification scheme would locate it on a continuum and thus serve to indicate what is intended (as well as what is *not* intended).

Values of the Taxonomy

We envisioned several major values arising from the attempt to order these desired outcomes. In the first instance, the actual sharing in the process of classifying educational objectives would help the members of the group *clarify* and tighten the "language of educational objectives." We were aware that all too frequently educational objectives are stated as meaningless platitudes and clichés. Some view them as an opportunity to use a type of prose found frequently in the superlatives employed by advertising men and the builders of political platforms. If, however, educational objectives are to give direction to the learning process and to determine the nature of the evidence to be used in appraising the effects of learning experiences, the terminology must become clear and meaningful.

It was hoped that the statement of an objective in similar terms by different workers would make possible a definite classification of that objective and would also permit exact inferences about the kinds of behaviors expected of students. The ideal, of course, would be educational objectives stated so clearly that the authors of the objective would know exactly what they meant and the readers of the objectives would have an equally clear idea of what was intended. While we never did quite expect to reach this ideal because of the difficulties in using language to communicate intentions, we did hope that it might be possible to devise a system of classification which would permit one to know almost exactly what is meant by a particular category. Thus, if the authors or readers of an objective should place it in a particular category, the consequences for learning experiences and evaluation would become relatively precise and clear.[1]

A second value to be derived from the creation of a classification scheme would be to provide a convenient system for describing and ordering test items, examination techniques, and evaluation instruments. We had found it difficult to exchange test material, primarily because of its tremendous bulk. Thus, an examiner at one institution who wished to use the material developed by examiners in other places had to do a great deal of reading before he could find a few items which were clearly relevant to his needs. If, however, test materials were classified as to content and objectives, one should be able to determine quickly what was available and useful for a particular task in examination development.

An even more important value we hoped to secure from the classification scheme was that of comparing and studying educational programs. If programs have similar objectives, do they involve similar or different learning experiences? The classifications could be used as tools in clarifying and organizing educational research results. What types of educational experiences produce what types of educational development? What types of educational development are well retained and what types are not?

[1] Throughout the two *Taxonomy* Handbooks, the term "educational objectives" refers to the objectives formulated by teachers, curriculum workers, etc. We clearly recognize that students also have educational objectives which are most influential in shaping the instructor's choice of teaching methods. Our concern, however, is with the choice of content and behavior which forms the structure of the planned curriculum and which provides a basis for evaluating the success of a given educational program.

What is the relation between intelligence and various types of educational progress? What is the transfer value of different kinds of educational outcomes? These are a few of the questions which we strive to understand through educational research. Through the Taxonomy we hoped to relate the results found in one educational situation to the results discovered in another. By this process we might be able to bring together the results of educational research so as to enable us to draw larger generalizations.

Finally, we were seeking something beyond a simple classification scheme. We envisioned the possibility that we might select principles of classifying educational outcomes which would reveal a real order among these outcomes. If such an order was confirmed by various types of observations and research findings, the order and principles of arrangement should be of value in the development of a theory of learning which would be relevant to the complex as well as simple types of human learning. At the very least, the discovery of some of the principles of ordering human-learning outcomes should define the types of findings that a useful theory of learning must be able to explain.

The Three Domains of the Taxonomy

Following our initial meeting, a series of meetings was held by a group of college and university examiners. At these meetings, which were in the nature of work sessions lasting two to four days, we began by creating a threefold division of educational objectives: cognitive, affective, and psychomotor. We found that most of the objectives stated by teachers in our own institutions, as well as those found in the literature, could be placed rather easily in one of three major domains or classifications:

1. *Cognitive:* Objectives which emphasize remembering or reproducing something which has presumably been learned, as well as objectives which involve the solving of some intellective task for which the individual has to determine the essential problem and then reorder given material or combine it with ideas, methods, or procedures previously learned. Cognitive objectives vary from simple recall of material learned to highly original and creative ways of combining and synthesizing new ideas and materials. We found that the largest proportion of educational objectives fell into this domain.

2. *Affective:* Objectives which emphasize a feeling tone, an emotion, or a degree of acceptance or rejection. Affective objectives vary from simple attention to selected phenomena to complex but internally consistent qualities of character and conscience. We found a large number of such objectives in the literature expressed as interests, attitudes, appreciations, values, and emotional sets or biases.

3. *Psychomotor:* Objectives which emphasize some muscular or motor skill, some manipulation of material and objects, or some act which requires a neuromuscular co-ordination. We found few such objectives in the literature. When found, they were most frequently related to handwriting and speech and to physical education, trade, and technical courses.

The reader will undoubtedly recognize that such a threefold division is as ancient as Greek philosophy and that philosophers and psychologists have repeatedly used similar tripartite organizations: cognition, conation, and feeling; thinking, willing, and acting; etc. Modern research on personality and learning raises serious questions about the value of these simple distinctions.

Basically, the question posed by modern behavioral science research is whether a human being ever does thinking without feeling, acting without thinking, etc. It seems very clear that each person responds as a "total organism" or "whole being" whenever he does respond. In spite of this, research on aptitudes and interest (Adkins and Kuder, 1940) does reveal quite small correlations between aptitudes and interests. Similarly, much of the research on the relations between cognitive achievement and attitudes and values shows them to be statistically independent. This is illustrated by Mayhew (1958), who reports little relationship between attitude changes and growth of knowledge in a college course. This does not mean that individuals with high aptitudes and interests do not exist, or that individuals with high achievements and "desirable" attitudes do not exist. What it does mean is that the relationship between these domains is too low to predict one type of response, effectively, from the other.

However, much more germane to our problem, which is that of classifying educational objectives, is that the teachers and curriculum workers who state objectives do make distinctions between problem solving and attitudes, between thinking and feeling, and between acting and thinking or feeling. These distinctions are accordingly reflected in our attempts to categorize objectives.

In addition, the evaluation of the outcomes of learning has involved very different techniques to appraise thinking, feeling, and acting; thus our distinctions are likely to be of service for the evaluation of school learning.

Finally, reconciliation between the classification of objectives and theories of personality and learning is likely to come in the ways of dealing with individual children and the interaction between teachers and students, rather than in the forcing of a set of classification procedures to agree with particular views about the functioning of human organisms.

We should note that any classification scheme represents an attempt to abstract and order phenomena and as such probably does some violence to the phenomena as commonly observed in natural settings. The value of these attempts to abstract and classify is in their greater power for organizing and controlling the phenomena. We believe the value of the present system of classification is likely to be in the greater precision with which objectives are likely to be stated, in the increased communicability of the objectives, and in the extent to which evaluation evidence will become available to appraise students' progress toward the objectives.

It was evident in our work that, although one could place an objective very readily in one of the three major domains or classes, no objective in one class was entirely devoid of some components of the other two classes. The domains evidently represent emphases and perhaps even biases in the statement of objectives. We hesitated to adopt this threefold division except on the practical grounds that objectives are so stated (and intended) that they fall rather easily into one of the three divisions.

Development and Use of the Taxonomy in the Cognitive Domain

Since the majority of objectives at the college and secondary level fell into the cognitive domain, the examiner group gave it top priority. We also found that most of our examinations for grading and evaluation purposes emphasized the objectives in this domain. Thus, the cognitive domain focused most directly on the objectives emphasized by our teachers and on the examination work being done by our examining staffs.

In the cognitive domain we found that many of the objectives had been developed with considerable precision as the result of much interaction between teachers and evaluators. Thus an objective such as "the development of skill in the interpretation of data" had been defined in detail by teachers and evaluators, and a sizable collection of techniques for appraising the extent to which students have developed this skill had been devised by examiners. Furthermore, we were able to find more than a thousand test questions and problems which had been developed to test various aspects of this one skill.

The equation "objective = behaviors = evaluation technique = test problems," has been so explicitly worked out for this objective that the developers of a classification scheme must accept the reality and meaningfulness of such an outcome of learning. That is, an objective has come to mean a particular set of behaviors, and the relation between behavior and the objective has been recognized by many workers in the field. Further, a particular set of evaluation techniques has come to be accepted as the appropriate way of appraising these behaviors, and even a definite set and variety of test problems have come to be accepted as valid indicators of the particular objective and its behaviors. The task for the classification scheme was where to put such an objective, and not how to discover and give meaning to this objective.

The group also found that, as a result of more than twenty years of work in evaluation, some major distinctions among cognitive objectives had already arisen. Thus, in their work the teachers and evaluators had made very sharp divisions between the remembering of information and problem solving in which the individual had to attack a problem new to him. Distinctions, although less clear, had grown up between information, problem solving, and creative or original discoveries and syntheses.

Starting, then, with a large list of cognitive objectives, behavioral definitions, and evaluation materials, the group explored various ways of ordering them. After considerable effort and thought it became apparent that the objectives (and corresponding behaviors and evaluation materials) differed in complexity. An objective such as "knowledge of specific facts" could be isolated and defined at one level of complexity. But at another level of complexity this objective became a part of another objective such as "the ability to apply principles." At one point the "knowledge of specific facts" was an end in its own right, while at a later point it became a part of, tool for, or means to, a larger or more complex objective.

After some experimentation with different arrangements, the *principle of complexity* was developed as the major ordering basis for the cognitive domain. A subcommittee was then set the task of sharpening the definitions of the different classes of the cognitive domain and finding illustrative objectives and evaluation examples which could be used to give clearer and more operational definitions to each objective.

The subcommittee came back with a set of definitions, a set of educational objectives, and a set of test problems, which they asked the larger group to test by matching the objectives and problems with the definitions. The result of this attempt to relate the three revealed where the definitions were inadequate, as well as some of the conditions required for classification of objectives and test material. Revision of definitions and repeated efforts at classification by small groups of workers enabled us to arrive eventually at a point where we believed the classification procedures and the definitions of classes and subclasses were communicable. That is, *communicability* was determined by the extent to which a group of competent workers could, after relatively little experience with the classification procedures, agree on the approximate placement of objectives, statements of behavior, and test materials.

Another check on the adequacy of the classification procedures was to determine whether it was *comprehensive.* Could we take new lists of objectives which we believed to be cognitive in nature and find places in the classification for each objective? We found that we rarely encountered an objective which could not be placed in one of the major classes within the cognitive domain, although we were not always certain that we could find an appropriate subclass within which to put it. Further work on the subclasses was done until we felt we had an adequate, although far from perfect, scheme for placing each new objective.

It was clear that we finally had a comprehensive method of defining and classifying cognitive educational objectives. However, we were seeking something more than a set of categories and definitions. We were hopeful that the order and arrangement of the classes and subclasses expressed a fundamental relation among the possible outcomes of education. We were of the view that the principle of complexity which had become our basis of arrangement was a reflection of the order of difficulty of the learning of the different objectives. Thus, a knowledge objective was presumably easier (and quicker) to achieve than a more complex type of analysis or synthesis objective. Perhaps, also, an analysis objective, once learned, would be retained longer than a knowledge or comprehension objective. It was partially out of temerity and partially out of hope and optimism that we entitled our work, *Taxonomy of Educational Objectives: Cognitive Domain.*

We have been criticized for the use of the word "taxonomy." Some critics contended that we did not have a true taxonomy but only a useful way of describing and defining classes of educational objectives. Less severe critics suggested that many of our readers would not understand what taxonomy meant and that the word would produce more confusion than was desirable. In any case, we have retained the term "taxonomy."

A true taxonomy is a set of classifications which are ordered and arranged on the basis of a single principle or on the basis of a consistent set of principles. Such a true taxonomy may be tested by determining whether it is in agreement with empirical evidence and whether the way in which the classifications are ordered corresponds to a real order among the relevant phenomena. The taxonomy must also be consistent with sound theoretical views available in the field. Where it is inconsistent, a way should be developed of demonstrating or determining which alternative is the most adequate one. Finally, a true taxonomy should be of value in pointing to phenomena yet to be discovered.

Whether or not the classification scheme presented in *Handbook I: Cognitive Domain* is a true taxonomy is still far from clear. There is some evidence that the more complex objectives are more difficult to learn than the less complex ones (Bloom, 1954b; Chausow, 1955; Dressel and Mayhew, 1954). There is evidence that the test questions intended to evaluate the objectives which fall in the higher (and more complex) parts of the cognitive domain are more difficult than the test questions intended to evaluate the less complex objectives.

Dressel and Mayhew's (1954) study suggests that significant growth in some of the more complex objectives occurs only when there are learning experiences in many parts of a curriculum devoted to these objectives. That is, the learning environment must give major emphasis to the more complex objectives if significant growth is to take place in these objectives.

Some of the research on lecture vs. discussion suggests that the knowledge objectives may be learned equally well under each type of learning situation (McKeachie, 1962). On the other hand, the types of problem solving represented in the higher classes of the *Taxonomy* require opportunities to practice the behavior and are apparently more easily learned when problem solving is emphasized in discussion, laboratory, and other learning situations in which individuals attempt to attack problems and are helped to see ways in which their problem solving may be improved.

Handbook I: Cognitive Domain has been used by teachers, students, and examination workers over a period of six years. Some have found the illustrative examination techniques of value as models and as examples of some of the better developments in examination construction. Others have found the illustrative objectives and the classes of objectives suggestive of a range of outcomes which they had not previously utilized in their own courses and educational programs. The *Taxonomy* has been of value in classifying test material for exchange among test workers and as a basis for reviewing and criticizing standardized tests (Dressel and Nelson, 1956; Buros, 1959; Morris, 1961). Without doubt, the renewed emphasis on the more complex objectives is attributable in some small measure to the existence and use of the *Taxonomy*.

Whether we have a true taxonomy or not, it is clear that *Handbook I: Cognitive Domain* has proved to be useful in some of the ways originally envisioned by the examiners responsible for developing it. It is to be hoped that new research will emerge which will determine more clearly whether the group has developed a *classification* scheme or a *taxonomic order*. Both are useful, but the latter would, of course, have the greater range of consequences for practical as well as theoretical work in education.

Beginning Work on the Affective Domain

The usefulness of the first Handbook and a variety of pressures have kept us aware of the need for completing the second Handbook on the affective domain. The group of examiners responsible for the development of the cognitive domain also felt great interest in and some responsibility for preparing the second volume. A subcommittee was delegated responsibility for working on various aspects of the domain. At least six working meetings were devoted to this task. Although some progress was made, we did not feel secure enough in our results to publish the reports produced at these meetings. Several difficulties beset this work. First, there was a lack of clarity in the statements of affective objectives that we found in the literature. Second, it was difficult to find an ordering principle as simple and pervasive as that of complexity, which worked so satisfactorily in the cognitive domain. Third, few of the examiners at the college level were convinced that the development of the affective domain would make much difference in their work or that they would find great use for it, when completed. There was no doubt that the affective domain represented a more difficult classification problem than the cognitive domain.

However, our failure to complete the affective-domain Handbook and our pessimism about the possibility of completing it satisfactorily was more than offset by the many letters we received from teachers, specialists in measurement and evaluation, and educational research workers asking when the second Handbook would be published. It was evident that we had dropped one shoe and that the tenants in the room below were waiting for the second shoe to fall. Perhaps this is an illustration of the principle of closure, in that an attempt had been made to order educational outcomes into three domains—cognitive, affective, and psychomotor—and that the original proposers of the scheme are to be held to the completion of the scheme, or else to a confession that it is unworkable.

Two of us who had been active in the original work on the classification of educational goals felt some special responsibility for the completion of the second Handbook. With the consent of the majority of the other members of the original committee of college and university examiners, we have assumed the task of preparing such a handbook. We have been aided by a group of critics (see page viii of the Preface) who have made suggestions after reading the first draft of the work. After seeing the first draft of the chapters in Part I and the category descriptions of Part II, Bertram B. Masia was persuaded to write the sections on testing of affective objectives in Part II of the Handbook. Since there have been no meetings of the examiners organization since 1957, they have not considered this manuscript as a group, and responsibility for the classification scheme must remain with us. We present it with some trepidation and full expectation of severe criticism from many quarters.

However, the value of this second Handbook is not likely to be determined by the amount of criticism we receive (or avoid). Rather, it is in its usefulness to teachers, evaluators, and curriculum workers. It is also in the extent to which it can help educators redress the erosion in the meaning and substance of affective objectives which has resulted from the greater emphasis on cognitive objectives. In the next chapter we shall try to describe the nature of the erosion which has taken place in the affective objectives and the task to which a meaningful and useful taxonomy of affective objectives must address itself.

CHAPTER 2

THE NEED FOR A CLASSIFICATION OF AFFECTIVE OBJECTIVES

Having suffered frustration and to some extent failure in our attempts to classify affective objectives, we were a bit surprised to find that many members of the original Taxonomy group still thought the task important and worth the effort to complete it. Why go ahead, however, with an effort which had thus far been so unproductive? In our attempt to face our own motivations we began to see more clearly a number of factors in this problem.

Limited Evaluation of Affective Objectives

One of the reasons the cognitive domain presented us with a more easily solvable problem than the affective domain was the tremendous wealth of evaluation material we found being used for grading and certifying student achievement. Faculty, examiners, administrators, and even students accept the need for and value of such material.

When we looked for evaluation material in the affective domain we found it usually in relation to some national educational research project or a sponsored local research project (for which a report had to be written). Only rarely did we find an affective evaluation technique used because a group of local teachers wanted to know whether students were developing in a particular way. It was evident that evaluation work for affective objectives was marginal and was done only when a very pressing question was raised by the faculty or when someone wished to do "educational" research.

It is not entirely fair to imply that evaluation of the attainment of affective objectives is completely absent from the regular activities of schools and teachers. Undoubtedly almost every teacher is on the alert for evidence of desirable interests, attitudes, and character development. However, most of this is the noting of unusual characteristics or dramatic developments when they are almost forced on the teacher's attention. What is missing is a systematic effort to collect evidence of growth in affective objectives which is in any way parallel to the very great and systematic efforts to evaluate cognitive achievement.

Erosion of Affective Objectives

We studied the history of several major courses at the general education level of college. Typically, we found that in the original statement of objectives there was frequently as much emphasis given to affective objectives as to cognitive objectives. Sometimes in the early years of the course some small attempt was made to secure evidence on the extent to which students were developing in the affective behaviors.

However, as we followed some of these courses over a period of ten to twenty years, we found a rather rapid dropping of the affective objectives from the statements about the course and an almost complete disappearance of efforts at appraisal of student growth in this domain.

It was evident to us that there is a characteristic type of *erosion* in which the original intent of a course or educational program becomes worn down to that which can be explicitly evaluated for grading purposes and that which can be taught easily through verbal methods (lectures, discussions, reading materials, etc.). There is a real shift in intent that comes with time. It may be true that it is easier to teach and evaluate cognitive objectives. But we really doubt that this is the sole determining influence and believe that a number of forces are responsible for the erosion of intentions.

School Grading and Affective Objectives

The failure to grade students' achievement on affective objectives accounts for a large portion of the erosion. Cognitive achievement is regarded as fair game for grading purposes. Examinations may include a great range of types of cognitive objectives, and teachers and examiners have little hesitation in giving a student a grade of A or F on the basis of his performance on these cognitive achievement examinations. In contrast, teachers and examiners do not regard it as appropriate to grade students with respect to their interests, attitude, or character development. To be sure, a student who is at one extreme on these affective objectives may be disciplined by the school authorities, while a student at the other extreme may be regarded so favorably by teachers that he receives whatever rewards and honors are available for the purpose (e.g., the teacher's attention, appointment to prestige classroom positions, etc.).

A considerable part of the hesitation in the use of affective measures for grading purposes stems from the inadequacy of the appraisal techniques and the ease with which a student may exploit his ability to detect the responses which will be rewarded and the responses which will be penalized. In contrast, it is assumed that a student who responds in the desirable way on a cognitive measure does indeed possess the competence which is being sampled. For instance, if we wish to determine whether a humanities course has resulted in "an interest in seeking and enjoying a wide variety of musical experiences," we may attempt to appraise the variety of musical experiences the student has voluntarily participated in prior to, during, and subsequent to the humanities course. We hesitate to trust the professed evidence that a student has developed such an interest, because we have difficulty in determining the difference between a natural or honest response and one that is made solely to please the teacher, and we may even have some question about the accuracy of the student's recall of such experiences. On the other hand, if our objective is "the development of the ability to become sensitive to and perceptive of different aspects of a musical work," we may present him with a series of musical selections which are likely to be unfamiliar to him. Then, by careful questioning, determine which elements he has perceived and which he has not. We would not hesitate to assign him a grade on the second objective, but we would have considerable hesitation about failing the student or giving him a high grade on the basis of our evidence on the first objective. However, though this difficulty with affective measures presents a series of technical problems, they could probably be solved with very substantial effort.

A much more serious reason for the hesitation in the use of affective measures for grading purposes comes from somewhat deeper philosophical and cultural values. Achievement, competence, productivity, etc., are regarded as public matters. Honors are awarded for high achievement, honor lists may be published by the Dean, and lists of National Merit Scholarship winners may be printed in newspapers. In contrast, one's beliefs, attitudes, values, and personality characteristics are more likely to be regarded as private matters, except in the most extreme instances already noted. My attitudes toward God, home, and family are private concerns, and this privacy is generally respected. My political attitudes are private; I may reveal them if I wish, but no one can force me to do so. In fact, my voting behavior is usually protected from public view. Each man's home is his castle, and his interests, values, beliefs, and personality may not be scrutinized unless he voluntarily gives permission to have them revealed. This public-private status of cognitive vs. affective behaviors is deeply rooted in the Judaeo-Christian religion and is a value highly cherished in the democratic traditions of the Western world.

Closely linked to this private aspect of affective behavior is the distinction frequently made between education and indoctrination in a democratic society. Education opens up possibilities for free choice and individual decision. Education helps the individual to explore many aspects of the world and even his own feelings and emotion, but choice and decision are matters for the individual. Indoctrination, on the other hand, is viewed as reducing the possibilities of free choice and decision. It is regarded as an attempt to persuade and coerce the individual to accept a particular viewpoint or belief, to act in a particular manner, and to profess a particular value and way of life. Gradually education has come to mean an almost solely cognitive examination of issues. Indoctrination has come to mean the teaching of affective as well as cognitive behavior. Perhaps a reopening of the entire question would help us to see more clearly the boundaries between education and indoctrination, and the simple dichotomy expressed above between cognitive and affective behavior would no longer seem as real as the rather glib separation of the two suggests.

Slow Attainment of Affective Objectives

Another cause of the erosion in affective objectives has to do with the immediacy of results. A particular item of information or a very specific skill is quickly learned and shows immediate results on cognitive examinations. Even more complex abilities may be learned in a one-semester or one-year course, and the evidences of the learning may be seen in the examination given at the end of the course. In contrast, interests, attitudes, and personality characteristics are assumed to develop relatively slowly and to be visible in appraisal techniques only over long periods of time, perhaps even years. Whether these assumptions are sound can only be revealed by much more evidence than is now available.

It is even possible that just the opposite may be true; namely, that affective behaviors undergo far more sudden transformations than do cognitive behaviors. What is even more probable is that certain objectives in the cognitive and affective domain may be quickly learned or developed, whereas other objectives in both domains may be developed only over a long period of time. Implicit in the *Taxonomy* is the assumption that objectives which fall into the first categories (e.g., *Knowledge, Receiving*) are likely to be learned more rapidly and more easily than objectives which fall into the later and "higher" categories (e.g., *Synthesis, Generalized set*). In any case, a useful classification of affective and cognitive objectives and behaviors would help to expose these assumptions about change (as well as the conditions required for change) in the different types of objectives, whether they be cognitive or affective.

Teaching for Affective Learning in Relation to Cognitive Learning

Before closing this discussion of causes of the erosion of affective objectives, we should point up the distinction between objectives as goals to be worked for directly and objectives which are assumed to be the by-products of other objectives (Sawin and Loree, 1959). For a long time it was assumed that if a student learned the information objectives of a course he would, as a direct consequence of this information learning, develop the problem-solving objectives in that course. Thus the teacher's responsibility was reduced to that of providing learning experiences to develop the information in students, and the examination was designed to appraise the students' progress toward the information objectives. As a result of the research and writings of Tyler (1934, 1951), Furst (1958), Dressel (1958), and others this belief in the "automatic" development of the higher mental processes is no longer widely held. However, there still persists an implicit belief that if cognitive objectives are developed, there will be a corresponding development of appropriate affective behaviors. Research summarized by Jacob (1957) raises serious questions about the tenability of this assumption. The evidence suggests that affective behaviors develop when appropriate learning experiences are provided for students much the same as cognitive behaviors develop from appropriate learning experiences.

The authors of this work hold the view that under some conditions the development of cognitive behaviors may actually destroy certain desired affective behaviors and that, instead of a positive relation between growth in cognitive and affective behavior, it is conceivable that there may be an inverse relation between growth in the two domains. For example, it is quite possible that many literature courses at the high-school and college levels instill knowledge of the history of literature and knowledge of the details of particular works of literature, while at the same time producing an aversion to, or at least a lower level of interest in, literary works. Clearly there is need for conclusive experimentation and research on the relations between the two domains. Here, again, the specificity which a taxonomy can introduce into both domains is likely to reveal conditions under which one conclusion is sound as well as point to situations where the opposite conclusion is tenable.

Perhaps one of the most dramatic events highlighting the need for progress in the affective domain was the publication of Jacob's *Changing Values in College* (1957). He summarizes a great deal of educational research at the college level and finds almost no evidence that college experiences produce a significant change in students' values, beliefs, or personality. Although he has been criticized for his methods, definitions, and assumptions, his critics have not responded by pointing up changes in the affective domain which he had overlooked. Jacob's work has stimulated a considerable amount of soul searching at the college level and is undoubtedly responsible for an increase in interest and research in this area. We must pay our respects to Jacob for increasing our own determination to complete this Handbook.

Clarification of Cognitive and Affective Objectives

More than two decades of work on cognitive objectives have produced specific and meaningful results. Few serious workers now use such terms as "critical thinking," "problem solving," or "higher mental processes" as statements of objectives. These terms may be used to describe large goals and aims of education, but in describing the objectives of a course with specific sequences of learning experiences, curriculum makers have more recently made use of terms like "application of principles," "interpretation of data," "skill in recognizing assumptions," etc. These terms are further defined behaviorally, enabling teachers to analyze an examination or evaluation technique to determine whether it does or does not appraise the kinds of educational outcomes they have specified. This greater precision in specifications has, of course, evolved from a considerable amount of interaction between teachers and evaluators. General statements of objectives have been gradually refined and restated until the operational consequences for evaluation instruments became explicit. Furthermore, the consequences of these objectives for the development of learning experiences have become more and more clear as the result of the operational definitions provided by statements of behavior and evaluation instruments. The effectiveness of learning experiences in helping students attain selected objectives has also become clearer through the use of appropriate evaluation instruments in educational research. Such research has stimulated efforts to develop learning theory and learning principles which deal more directly with these highly specific educational objectives. All this is not an attempt to describe a Utopian situation in which cognitive objectives, learning experiences, and evaluation techniques have been developed so well that little further work is now needed. Far from this, we have barely scratched the surface of the tremendous potential for clarification and development of cognition.

However, the situation with respect to affective objectives is so primitive that little in the way of meaning is at present conveyed by statements of objectives. For example, here are six objectives selected from the literature, which purport to state outcomes in the affective domain:

1. The student should develop an attitude of faith in the power of reason and in the methods of experiment and discussion.

2. The student should develop attitudes of intelligent self-criticism in matters of effective expression and correct form of writing.

3. The student should develop an appreciation for the rights and feelings of others.

4. The student should have deep wells of feeling that manifest themselves not only in a passionate hatred of injustice, a "divine discontent," and an unwillingness to be a passive bystander in the presence of violently pressing social issues, but also in active and joyous identification of his own happiness with the larger social good.

5. The student should become interested in good books.

6. The student should develop an appreciation of classical music.

It will be noted that each of these states a general term like "interest," "attitude," or "appreciation" followed by an object such as books, music, people, etc. What is meant by "interest" may range from simply knowing that the object exists to a passionate devotion to this type of object or activity. For example, some possible interpretations of objective 5 may be the following:

The student should be able to distinguish between good books and not-so-good books.

The student should want to know more about what makes a book good.

The student should read an increasing number of books which experts classify as good.

The student should express a desire to read more good books.

The student should purchase good books for his personal library.

An evaluator attempting to develop an evaluation instrument to appraise growth toward objective 5 could infer almost anything he desired and construct the instrument accordingly. However, in that case the specification of the objectives of instruction would pass from the teachers to the examiners. This would represent a shift in control of instruction and outcomes from the teachers responsible for the learning experiences to the evaluators who devise the instruments for appraising the results of instruction. We regard this as an undesirable shift, since it places educational direction (and control) in the hands of a small number of instrument makers. Furthermore, it is likely that those teachers who, through vague statements of objectives, have yielded control over objectives to the examiners will not make major contributions to the development of learning experiences which will enable students to grow in the ways specified by the objectives.

The Contributions of a Taxonomy of Affective Objectives

If affective objectives and goals are to be realized, they must be defined clearly; learning experiences to help the student develop in the desired direction must be provided; and there must be some systematic method for appraising the extent to which students grow in the desired ways.

It is our hope that the *Taxonomy* will be of service in defining more clearly the objectives in this domain. If it does nothing more, it will serve to indicate that many of the present objectives in this domain are so general as to be meaningless.

It is our hope also that the *Taxonomy* will help teachers become aware of the techniques which are available for appraising growth of students toward various categories of objectives and for assessing other affective changes, whether intended or not. Perhaps this will further stimulate the development of better methods of evaluation in this domain.

Finally, it is our hope that the *Taxonomy* will provide a bridge for further communication among teachers and between teachers and evaluators, curriculum research workers, psychologists, and other behavioral scientists. As this communication process develops, it is likely that the "folklore" which we have presented in the beginning of this chapter can be replaced by a somewhat more precise understanding of how affective behaviors develop, how and when they can be modified, and what the school can and cannot do to develop them in particular forms.

CHAPTER 3

THE BASIS FOR AFFECTIVE-DOMAIN CLASSIFICATION

THE SEARCH FOR AN AFFECTIVE CONTINUUM

Perhaps the most difficult part of the task of building the affective domain of the *Taxonomy* was the search for a continuum that would provide a means of ordering and relating the different kinds of affective behavior. It was presumed that the affective domain, like the cognitive, would be structured in a hierarchical order such that each category of behavior would assume achievement of the behaviors categorized below it. But it did not appear likely that the principles of "simple to complex" and "concrete to abstract" would provide as appropriate a basis for structuring the affective domain as they had provided for the cognitive domain. Some additional construct had to be found.

An analysis of affective objectives was undertaken to determine their unique characteristics. It was hoped that among these we would find what was needed to structure an affective continuum. Combined with the structuring principles from the cognitive domain, we might then expect the affective structure to begin with simple, concrete, less pervasive behaviors having a little of some characteristic as yet unspecified. These levels would be the building blocks for the more complex, abstract, and pervasive behaviors having much more of this unspecified characteristic. The problem was to define the then unspecified characteristic and the principle by which it would structure the continuum.

As has already been indicated in previous chapters, the materials from which this continuum was to be educed were the objectives dealing with interests, attitudes, values, appreciation, and adjustment. These terms were all found to have too wide a variety of meanings to serve, themselves, as the focal points through which to construct a continuum. But an analysis of the range of meanings used for each of these terms did lead to an understanding of the characteristics of the affective domain which would have to be both encompassed and ordered. It also led to the formulation of the principle needed to establish a continuum.

This analysis found, for instance, that objectives dealing with interests describe behavior ranging all the way from the student's merely *being aware* that a given phenomenon exists (so that he will at least give it his attention when it is present) through behavior where he is increasingly willing to attend and respond to a phenomenon, to behavior where he is expected to *avidly seek* out the phenomenon in question and to be totally absorbed in it. Throughout the range, it is expected that the student will *feel positively* toward the phenomenon, but at the "high interest" end he is expected to be fairly enamored of it.

The term "attitude" was also found to include objectives with a wide range of behaviors. On the one hand, it is used to describe the involvement of the student who is willing to grant that he has a *positive feeling about something* when he is asked about it. At the other extreme, it is expected that his commitment is such that *he goes out of his way* to express it and even seeks instances in which he can communicate it to others. Objectives dealing with attitudes frequently require the individual to have *a clear conception* of his attitude which he can verbalize.

When we speak of an individual as holding a value, the same range of behavior described for attitudes comes into play. Further, both the terms "attitude" and "value" may refer to behavior which has either rather specific referents as its object, e.g., one's next-door neighbors, or much more general and pervasive referents, e.g., all minority groups. In the latter instance, although the terms "attitude" and "value" are still usually employed, the behavior is often better described as a bundle of attitudes *organized* into an attitude cluster or a value complex.

The term "appreciation," like "interest," may refer to such a simple behavior as a person's being aware of a phenomenon and *being able to perceive it.* It may require that the individual be able to verbalize it (in which instance it may become almost a cognitive rather than an affective objective). It may require only that the individual *experience a pleasant feeling* when he perceives the phenomenon.

Of the terms analyzed, the widest range of meanings is probably accorded the term "adjustment." Central to any definition of adjustment is an *interrelation of one aspect* of the person *with another* in such a way that within this organization some kind of balancing may take place. The term may refer to such behaviors as appear in the social interaction between two persons, or it may *refer to one's whole outlook on life.* It may refer to the internal balancing of self-concept and self-ideal or to the balancing of overt behavior with some role concept.

If the discussion so far does not completely describe the range of behavior in the objectives of the affective domain, it does at least outline its major components. What guideposts for an affective continuum can be gleaned from them? In the paragraphs above, material has been italicized which seemed to indicate the behavioral components which must be provided for in the affective-domain structure. From these it is clear that we must first provide a level at which the stimulus is attended to so it can enter the organism's life and be perceived. This would cover the less complex aspects of interest and appreciation objectives.

Similarly, we must provide a range of levels describing the extent to which the individual interacts with the phenomenon and the basis on which he does it: does he do it only when the situation presses on him so that some behavior is evoked, or does he go out of his way to display this interaction? This would provide for some of the behaviors implied in the objectives calling for development of interests and appreciation and the less complex attitudes.

Provision must be made at some point in the continuum for the first appearance of the emotional quality which is an important distinguishing feature of the appreciation, attitude, value, and adjustment objectives in the affective domain. Further, we need to provide the range of emotion from neutrality through mild to strong emotion, probably of a positive, but possibly also of a negative, kind.

From the description of attitudes, values, and adjustment, it is clear that the continuum must provide for the organization and interrelation of values and attitudes and for whatever steps accompany or are prerequisite to such organization.

Finally, the range of behaviors to be encompassed and the way these are organized into value systems and philosophies of life suggest that the continuum should provide for various levels of organization to be delineated.

At one stage in our work in this domain it was hoped that by appropriately delimited definitions of such terms as interest, attitude, value, etc., we could build the components into a string of guideposts tied to the common terms in the field. But such definitions were difficult to devise, and their meanings tended to drift into the connotations and denotations which these terms encompassed in common parlance.[1] When we abandoned this, we tried to fit the components into the various theories of learning and theories of personality which were extant in the field. While we were able to find the components in almost all the formal theories, we did not find any one theory which structured the components into a single continuum and which sufficiently clarified the meanings of a representative range of objectives chosen from the literature.

The more we carefully studied the components, however, the clearer it became that a continuum might be derived by appropriately ordering them. Thus the continuum progressed from a level at which the individual is merely *aware* of a phenomenon, being *able to perceive it*. At a next level he is *willing to attend* to phenomena. At a next level he *responds* to the phenomena with a *positive feeling*. Eventually he may feel strongly enough to *go out of his way* to respond. At some point in the process he conceptualizes his behavior and feelings and *organizes* these conceptualizations into a structure. This structure grows in complexity as *it becomes his life outlook*.

This ordering of the components seemed to describe a process by which a given phenomenon or value passed from a level of bare awareness to a position of some power to guide or control the behavior of a person. If it passed through all the stages in which it played an increasingly important role in a person's life, it would come to dominate and control certain aspects of that life

[1]Readers interested in gaining a perspective on the matter of definitions as they relate to this effort should examine Chapter 1, "Definitions in Education," in Scheffler (1960). In Scheffler's terms we initially tried to obtain descriptive definitions of common terms which would permit their use to structure a continuum. We found we could do this only if we gave these terms noninventive stipulative definitions, and we feared the stipulations attached to these definitions would be lost when the terms were used outside the context of the *Taxonomy* structure. An examination of the category headings will show that we finally sought less commonly used terms, where, though we were still using noninventive stipulative definitions, the definitions given these terms and their descriptive definitions were more congruent.

as it was absorbed more and more into the internal controlling structure. This process or continuum seemed best described by a term which was heard at various times in our discussions and which has been used similarly in the literature: "internalization." This word seemed an apt description of the process by which the phenomenon or value successively and pervasively become a part of the individual.

When we tried this concept as an organizing principle, we found we were able to construct a meaningful continuum. When we tried it with objectives, we found it helpful in delimiting and describing them and in classifying them into this structure. Our method of choice of an organizing structure was a combination of analytic and pragmatic criteria. The process termed "internalization" was chosen because it encompassed and combined the components which were present when we analyzed the behaviors implied by objectives belonging in the domain. It gave an ordering to these components which appeared to be reasonably parallel to some of our theories about how learning takes place with affective objectives. It helped to define operationally the kinds of tasks a teacher faces in this domain. It appeared to provide a means for cutting through the tangle of conflicting and inadequate learning theories without tying the structure to any one of them. It was consistent with the behavioral point of view of education which places the focus of learning within the individual, and it constructed a continuum of his behavior. It helped to simplify and clarify the meaning of both terse and lengthy complex affective objectives if we analyzed them from this point of view.

Once we decided to adopt it, our problems became (1) to define more completely what was meant by the word "internalization," in relation both to some of its previous uses and to similar terms used by psychologists and educators (pp. 29–33 of this chapter); (2) to describe the way it appears in the structuring of an affective continuum and the way that continuum can be arbitrarily but meaningfully divided into stages or levels (pp. 33–35 of this chapter and the sections of Part II of this Handbook which give detailed descriptions of the categories); (3) to relate the affective continuum to commonly used affective terms (pp. 36–38 of this chapter); (4) to test the structure against some research evidence (pp. 38–43 of this chapter).

INTERNALIZATION: ITS NATURE

The description of the process of internalization is not a product of any one theory or point of view. As we see it, it is not a new concept but a useful combination of old ones. English and English (1958) define it as "incorporating something within the mind or body; adopting as one's own the ideas, practices, standards, or values of another person or of society" (p. 272).

English and English's definition of internalization as "incorporating . . . within [oneself]" or "adopting as one's own" epitomizes the major aspect of internalization. As viewed in the *Taxonomy,* however, internalization may occur in varying degrees, depending on the extent to which there is an adoption of others' values. Thus in the *Taxonomy* internalization is viewed as a process through which there is at first an incomplete and tentative adoption of only the overt manifestations of the desired behavior and later a more complete adoption.

English and English note that the term is a close relative of the term "socialization," which, though it is "often used as a synonym . . . [properly means] . . . conformity in outward behavior without necessarily accepting the values." They define socialization as "the process whereby a person . . . acquires sensitivity to social stimuli . . . and learns to get along with, and to behave like, others in his group or culture" (p. 508). They also note that it is a major part of the acquisition of personality.

English and English's concept of socialization helps to define a portion of the content of the affective domain—that which is internalized—as well as the first part of the process itself. But even as a description of the content of the affective domain this definition must be interpreted broadly, since "sensitivity to social stimuli" must include the arts as well as others' behavior.

This definition suggests that the culture is perceived as the controlling force in the individual's actions. It is true that the internalization of the prevailing values of the culture describes the bulk of contemporary objectives. But it is equally true that our schools, in their roles as developers of individualism and as change agents in the culture, are not solely concerned with conformity. Internalization as defined in the *Taxonomy* provides equally for the development of both conformity and nonconformity, as either role pervades individual behavior. The term "internalization," by referring to the process through which values, attitudes, etc., in general are acquired, is thus broader than socialization, which refers only to the acceptance of the contemporary value pattern of the society.[2]

An old educational axiom states that "growth occurs from within." The term "internalization" refers to this inner growth which takes place as there is "acceptance by the individual of the attitudes, codes, principles, or sanctions that become a part of himself in forming value judgments or in determining his conduct" (Good, 1959, definition of "internalization," p. 296). This growth takes place in different ways. One of these ways is the increased emotional impact of the experience. At the lowest levels of the internalization continuum there is little emotion in the behavior. At this end the individual is mainly just perceiving the phenomenon. At the middle levels, emotional response is a recognized and critical part of the behavior as the individual actively responds. As the behavior becomes completely internalized and routine, this emotion decreases and is not a regular part of most responses.

Another aspect of the growth is the extent to which external control by the environment yields to inner control as one ascends the continuum. Thus at the lowest end of the continuum, inner control serves only to direct attention. At higher levels, inner control produces appropriate responses, but only at the bidding of an external authority. At still higher levels, inner control produces the appropriate response even in the absence of an external authority. Indeed at still higher levels, these responses are produced consistently despite obstacles and barriers.[3]

---

[2]Internalization of socially disapproved as well as socially approved behavior is possible and does occur. But except as such behavior is used as an educational goal or objective, there is no attempt to encompass it in this framework. Thus, in general, fear, regression, and the various forms of social maladjustment, though of concern to many psychological theorists, lie outside the scope of educational objectives and therefore are not encompassed by the *Taxonomy*. On rare occasions, however, some "negative" emotion such as disgust or indignation (e.g., when racial equality is not observed) or fear (e.g., of bodily injury when safety rules are violated) may appear in an educational objective. It may be restated in its more usual form to stress the positive side (e.g., commitment to the observation of racial equality, conformance to safety rules). By such restatement, the present structure could be used for either positively or "negatively" oriented objectives.

[3]As can be noted by reference to Appendix A or Part II, the titles of the categories imply this change in direction of control. A lower level is titled *Responding*, thus indicating that the individual is reacting to an outer control. The next level is titled *Valuing* to indicate that the control is becoming internal.

These different aspects of growth suggest that it is probable that the internalization continuum is multidimensional. Certainly it has a simple-to-complex aspect as well as a concrete-to-abstract one. There is the external-to-internal control transition. There is an emotional component that increases up to a point on the continuum. Finally there are the conscious-to-unconscious aspects and the cognitive aspects of organization of attitudinal components. (The latter are considered in more detail in the next chapter.)

Any continuum can be more easily and precisely defined if it is unidimensional. But it seems unlikely that we can account for affective phenomena with a unidimensional continuum at this state of our knowledge. We have found the term "intelligence" an extremely useful concept, even though it may be argued that it is multidimensional. It is hoped that internalization will prove a similarly useful basis for this structure, even though it, too, is probably multidimensional.

Further clues to the meaning of internalization can be found in its previous usages. For instance, Pitts (1961) uses the term apparently to replace the term "identification," where the latter refers to one's taking on the values and attitudes of another. Thus, in his description of Freud's concept of superego differentiation, he notes that the child internalizes the father figure to form the superego as a way of resolving the pressures and exigencies of the family. He notes that "major collectivities such as the church, state and army can replace the parental figures that the growing adolescent finds wanting in omnipotence or omniscience" (p. 687). We might add the school to this list as one of those collectivities which replace the parental figure and thus modify the internalized pattern of values. The school furthers the differentiation of the superego, providing additional models to replace the parent and, as does any institution, using other means besides modeling to provide for attitude and value development. Thus, the term "internalization" as used by Pitts in the description of superego development describes a way of looking at internalization which is consistent with the way the term is used in the *Taxonomy*.

Kelman (1958) used the term in describing a theory of attitude change. He distinguished three different processes (compliance, identification, and internalization) by which an individual accepts influence or conforms. These three processes are defined as follows:

> Compliance can be said to occur when an individual accepts influence because he hopes to achieve a favorable reaction from another person or group. He adopts the induced behavior not because he believes in its content but because he expects to gain specific rewards or approval and avoid specific punishments or disapproval by conforming. . . .
>
> Identification can be said to occur when an individual accepts influence because he wants to establish or maintain a satisfying relationship to another person or group (e.g. teacher or other school authority). . . . The individual actually believes in the responses which he adopts through identification. . . . The satisfaction derived from identification is due to the act of conforming as such.
>
> Internalization can be said to occur when an individual accepts influence because the content of the induced behavior—the ideas and actions of which it is composed—is intrinsically rewarding. He adopts the induced behavior because it is congruent with his value system. . . . Behavior adopted in this fashion tends to be integrated with the individual's existing values. Thus, the satisfaction derived from internalization is due to the content of the new behavior.[4]

The *Taxonomy* as a categorization of teacher goals is less concerned with the particular teaching process by which a kind of behavior is attained than is Kelman. But it does recognize the different behavioral products Kelman describes. The *Taxonomy* uses the term "internalization" to encompass all three of Kelman's terms, recognizing them as different stages in the internalization process. Thus, Kelman's "compliance" corresponds to a very early level on the internalization continuum at which the pupil complies with expectations without commitment to them. Kelman's "identification" is farther along in the internalization process and so is treated in the middle stages of the continuum. At these points the individual responds with the behavior desired, gaining some satisfaction from this response and accepting the values implied in the behavior—or as Kelman says, "actually believing" in them. Kelman's use of the term "internalization" refers to the end product of the educational and the internalization process: a person has accepted certain values, attitudes, interests, etc. into his system and is guided by these regardless of surveillance or salience of an influencing agent, be it teacher, principal, or others. The person acts as he does because to do so is in itself satisfying to him. As would be expected, this kind of behavior is described at the topmost end of the continuum. There the person is described as responding with commitment: accepting a value into his system, organizing that system, and developing a value complex that guides his behavior.

[4] Kelman, 1958, p. 53.

Thus, the *Taxonomy* uses the term "internalization" more broadly than does Kelman, referring to a process including a number of stages of internalization, where he refers to an internalized system as an end product.

Perhaps the best understanding of how the term is used in the *Taxonomy* is gained by referring to the structure itself.

Internalization as it Appears in the Taxonomy Structure

The process of internalization can be described by summarizing the continuum at successive levels as they appear in the *Affective Domain Taxonomy.* The process begins when the attention of the student is captured by some phenomenon, characteristic, or value. As he pays attention to the phenomenon, characteristic, or value, he differentiates it from the others present in the perceptual field. With differentiation comes a seeking out of the phenomenon as he gradually attaches emotional significance to it and comes to value it. As the process unfolds he relates this phenomenon to other phenomena to which he responds that also have value. This responding is sufficiently frequent so that he comes to react regularly, almost automatically, to it and to other things like it. Finally the values are interrelated in a structure or view of the world, which he brings as a "set" to new problems.

Even from this abstract description it can be seen that the internalization process represents a continuous modification of behavior from the individual's being aware of a phenomenon to a pervasive outlook on life that influences all his actions.

While this description of the process seemed reasonably satisfactory, if a hierarchical structure was to be provided and more adequate description of the process developed, it was clear that the continuum needed to be divided into steps or stages. In so far as possible, when this was done, the breaking points between steps were located where there appeared to be some kind of transition, such as the addition of a new component or kind of activity. Since the boundaries of the categories are completely arbitrary and can be defended only on pragmatic grounds, it is possible that later work may suggest that other breaking points would be more satisfactory. The divisions between major categories have proved quite useful in the analysis of objectives. We feel more sure of the major divisions than of the subcategories, some of which appear to be easier to delineate than others.

The steps in the process and their description are given in detail in Part II and are summarized in Appendix A. They are reviewed here to acquaint the reader with them and to show the parallel between the description of internalization which has been developed and the steps and levels into which it has been arbitrarily divided.

We begin with the individuals being aware of the stimuli which initiate the affective behavior and which form the context in which the affective behavior occurs. Thus, the lowest category is 1.0 *Receiving*. It is subdivided into three categories. At the 1.1 *Awareness* level, the individual merely has his attention attracted to the stimuli (e.g., he develops some consciousness of the use of shading to portray depth and lighting in a picture).[5] The second subcategory, 1.2 *Willingness to receive*, describes the state in which he has differentiated the stimuli from others and is willing to give it his attention (e.g., he develops a tolerance for bizarre uses of shading in modern art). At 1.3 *Controlled or selected attention* the student looks for the stimuli (e.g., he is on the alert for instances where shading has been used both to create a sense of three-dimensional depth and to indicate the lighting of the picture; or he looks for picturesque words in reading).

At the next level, 2.0 *Responding*, the individual is perceived as responding regularly to the affective stimuli. At the lowest level of responding, 2.1 *Acquiescence in responding*, he is merely complying with expectations (e.g., at the request of his teacher, he hangs reproductions of famous paintings in his dormitory room; he is obedient to traffic rules). At the next higher level, 2.2 *Willingness to respond*, he responds increasingly to an inner compulsion (e.g., voluntarily looks for instances of good art where shading, perspective, color, and design have been well used, or has an interest in social problems broader than those of the local community). At 2.3 *Satisfaction in response* he responds emotionally as well (e.g., works with clay, especially in making pottery for personal pleasure). Up to this point he has differentiated the affective stimuli; he has begun to seek them out and to attach emotional significance and value to them.

---

[5]This same objective is successively modified to carry it through many of the levels of the continuum. Readers who would like a fuller description of the reasoning behind the classification of this objective at any level should turn to pages 65–68 in Chapter 5, where the same example is used and its development through the hierarchy is explained in detail.

As the process unfolds, the next levels of 3.0 *Valuing* describe increasing internalization, as the person's behavior is sufficiently consistent that he comes to hold a value: 3.1 *Acceptance of a value* (e.g., continuing desire to develop the ability to write effectively and hold it more strongly), 3.2 *Preference for a value* (e.g., seeks out examples of good art for enjoyment of them to the level where he behaves so as to further this impression actively), and 3.3 *Commitment* (e.g., faith in the power of reason and the method of experimentation).

As the learner successively internalizes values he encounters situations for which more than one value is relevant. This necessitates organizing the values into a system, 4.0 *Organization.* And since a prerequisite to interrelating values is their conceptualization in a form which permits organization, this level is divided in two: 4.1 *Conceptualization of a value* (e.g., desires to evaluate works of art which are appreciated, or to find out and crystallize the basic assumptions which underlie codes of ethics) and 4.2 *Organization of a value system* (e.g., acceptance of the place of art in one's life as one of dominant value, or weighs alternative social policies and practices against the standards of public welfare).

Finally, the internalization and the organization processes reach a point where the individual responds very consistently to value-laden situations with an interrelated set of values, a structure, a view of the world. The *Taxonomy* category that describes this behavior is 5.0 *Characterization by a value or value complex,* and it includes the categories 5.1 *Generalized set* (e.g., views all problems in terms of their aesthetic aspects, or readiness to revise judgments and to change behavior in the light of evidence) and 5.2 *Characterization* (e.g., develops a consistent philosophy of life).

Stripped of their definitions, the category and subcategory titles appear in sequence as follows (see also Appendix A):

1.0 Receiving (attending)
   1.1 Awareness
   1.2 Willingness to receive
   1.3 Controlled or selected attention
2.0 Responding
   2.1 Acquiescence in responding
   2.2 Willingness to respond
   2.3 Satisfaction in response
3.0 Valuing
   3.1 Acceptance of a value
   3.2 Preference for a value
   3.3 Commitment (conviction)
4.0 Organization
   4.1 Conceptualization of a value
   4.2 Organization of a value system
5.0 Characterization by a value or value complex
   5.1 Generalized set
   5.2 Characterization

Relation of the Affective-Domain Structure to Common Affective Terms

As was noted in the beginning of this chapter, the analysis of such commonly used terms as interest, attitude, appreciation, and value showed each of them to have a wide range of meanings. When we examined the range of meanings for any one term and compared this range to the *Taxonomy* structure we found that each term generally took on meanings over a section of the internalization continuum. Figure 1 illustrates this.

Thus, objectives were found where interpretation of the term "interest" ranged all the way from the student's being aware that a phenomenon exists to the behavior of avidly seeking a phenomenon. This is shown in Figure 1 by the line marked "Interest" extending from the *Taxonomy* category of 1.1 *Awareness* to 3.2 *Preference for a value.* Apparently the term "interest" typically describes behavior that would be classified at the lower levels of the *Taxonomy.* Rarely would it be interpreted as describing a behavior we would describe as *Commitment* or higher.

Interpretation of the term "appreciation" as it appears in objectives shows that it may refer to such simple behavior as the person's being willing to attend to certain aspects of a phenomenon, to his feeling a response to some stimulus, or to his showing a preference for certain behavior or stimuli. Thus, appreciation would not be interpreted typically as including the behaviors at the lowest levels of the *Taxonomy* nor at the highest. The line in Figure 1 shows the segment of the continuum which appears to include the bulk of its range of meanings.[6]

Similarly when we examined the range of interpretations given to the terms "attitude" and "value" in educational objectives, we found they ranged from situations where the student was expected to display a particular behavior, especially with a certain amount of emotion (enthusiasm, warmth, or even disgust, if appropriate), to situations in which he might go out of his way to display the value or to communicate to others about it. Thus the lines in Figure 1 for these terms extend from 2.2 *Willingness to respond* to 4.1 *Conceptualization of a value.*

---

[6]Appreciation is sometimes interpreted to mean that the student can describe that aspect of a phenomenon (e.g., a dance) that he appreciates. In this respect the line should extend to 4.1 *Conceptualization of a value.* Yet, rarely does an appreciation objective connote a commitment to a value. This anomaly is discussed further in the description of the 4.0 category in Part II.

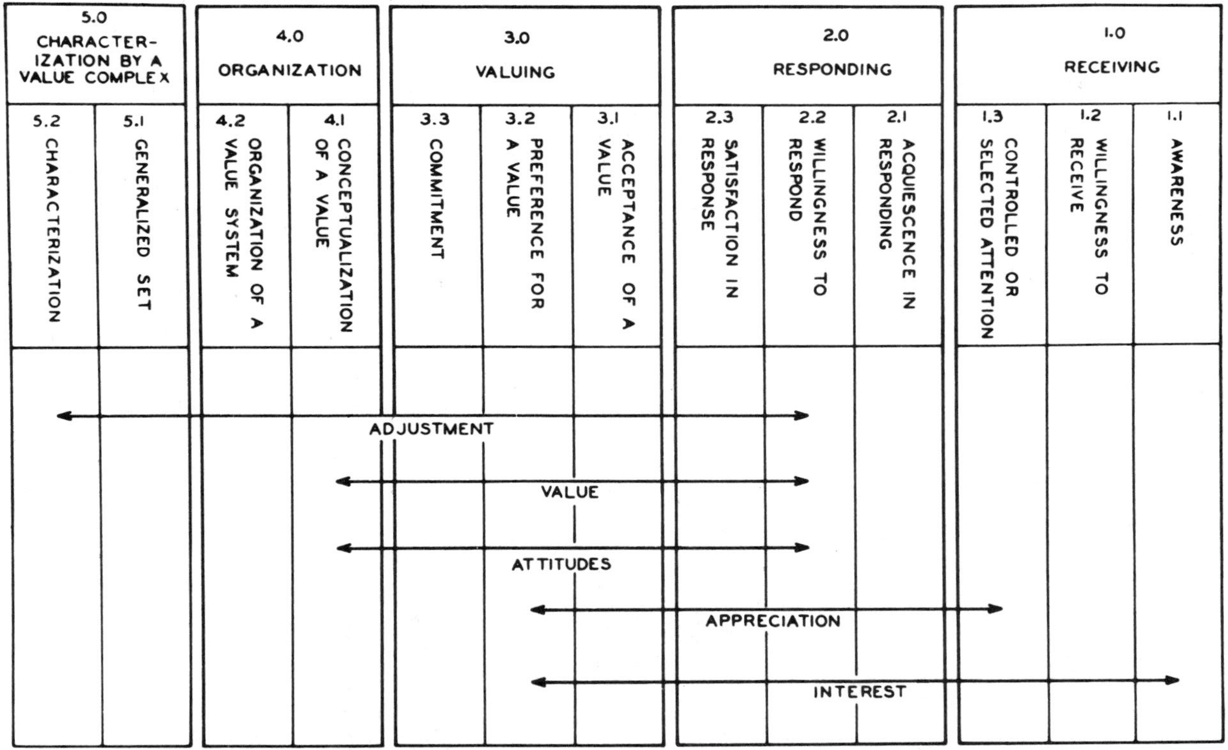

5.0 CHARACTERIZATION BY A VALUE COMPLEX
5.2 CHARACTERIZATION
5.1 GENERALIZED SET
4.0 ORGANIZATION
4.2 ORGANIZATION OF A VALUE SYSTEM
4.1 CONCEPTUALIZATION OF A VALUE
3.0 VALUING
3.3 COMMITMENT
3.2 PREFERENCE FOR A VALUE
3.1 ACCEPTANCE OF A VALUE
2.0 RESPONDING
2.3 SATISFACTION IN RESPONSE
2.2 WILLINGNESS TO RESPOND
2.1 ACQUIESCENCE IN RESPONDING
1.0 RECEIVING
1.3 CONTROLLED OR SELECTED ATTENTION
1.2 WILLINGNESS TO RECEIVE
1.1 AWARENESS
ADJUSTMENT
VALUE
ATTITUDES
APPRECIATION
INTEREST

FIGURE 1. The range of meaning typical of commonly used affective terms measured against the *Taxonomy* continuum.

The term "adjustment" appeared to take on a range of meanings, from a simple display of appropriate behavior in social interaction to the interrelation of one aspect of self to another—one's outlook on life. Thus, the line indicating its range of meanings extends from 2.2 *Willingness to respond* through 5.2 *Characterization.* It has the widest potential range of meanings of any of the terms, extending nearly across the entire range of taxonomic categories.

Several points with respect to this figure are worth noting. All the terms overlap one another in meaning in the middle range of the *Taxonomy* continuum. No specificity can be gained by replacing one term by another in this range, and possibilities for confusion are great.

A corollary of this observation is that no term (e.g., attitude) uniquely describes its entire segment of the continuum. Every term is overlapped by at least one other term for a major portion of that part of the continuum it describes.

Only the terms "interest" and "adjustment," at the lower and upper extremes, are not overlapped by another term for a portion of the continuum they include. In the objectives we have analyzed, "interest" appears to be used more often to describe behavior toward the middle range of the continuum than where it might be used with unique meaning, at the lowest extreme. "Adjustment," on the other hand, most frequently does refer in these objectives to the more complex kinds of behavior described in the upper levels of the *Taxonomy* to which it alone extends. In this respect, despite the range over which it is used, in its most frequent application it is intended to have a nearly unique meaning.

Finally, the figure indicates the increase in precision which it is hoped that the use of the affective continuum can achieve if its terms replace those in common use. For instance, the behavior involved in an "interest" objective could be given increased specificity if the objective were defined by placing it in one of the eight *Taxonomy* categories typically embraced by the term "interest."

The Relation of Internalization to the Development of Conscience

As indicated earlier, the process of socialization, with its development of behavioral controls, is a topic with which the affective domain is much involved. It seemed appropriate to compare the internalization continuum with the development of conscience.

The operation of conscience as defined by English and English (1958) is "the more or less integrated functioning of a person's system of moral values..." (p. 111). They further state that "the superego...is conceived in psychoanalysis as functioning substantially in the same way as conscience." Superego development is conceived as "...the incorporation of the moral standards of society..." (p. 535). Internalization (incorporating as one's own) is thus a critical element in superego development and in the development of conscience. Therefore the levels of the *Taxonomy* should describe successive levels of goal setting appropriate to superego development. English and English's definition, specifically pointing to the integrated functioning of a system, highlights a central emphasis of the upper categories of the affective domain, the integration and interrelation of a person's values into a system.

There have been a number of expositions of the development of conscience or the superego. One test of the *Taxonomy* would be a comparison of its levels with those found empirically or postulated theoretically for superego and conscience development. We would not necessarily expect to find a one-to-one correspondence between developmental stages and the *Taxonomy* since the former describes what stages, whether desirable or undesirable, are perceived to actually exist, whereas the *Taxonomy* is concerned only with teachers' positively stated goals or objectives. Nonetheless, if one limited oneself to the positive aspects of the developmental stages, one would expect some correspondence.

One of the most comprehensive of the relevant recent investigations with which the *Taxonomy* might be compared is the Moral-Character Study of Prairie City reported by Peck and Havighurst (1960). These authors found five types or stages of character development, which closely follow the stages of psychosocial maturation described by the Freudian theory of personality development. Their stages were named the amoral, expedient, conforming, irrational-conscientious, and rational-altruistic types.[7] The type names are largely self-explanatory.

[7] The conforming and the irrational-conscientious types are alternatives at the same stage of maturity. Peck and Havighurst recognize that persons are not likely to be pure types at any stage of development, but that a type of behavior may predominate. They also note that not all persons reach the point in maturity where rational-altruistic behavior predominates. In particular, many are fixated at the conforming level as Riesman (1961), among others, has noted.

The amoral type has an infantlike inability to control himself in social situations. As such, he does not represent a goal of teaching and is a stage below any of the *Taxonomy* levels. The expedient type "conforms in order to avoid adult punishment or disapproval.... If the punishments have been impressive enough, he may have internalized a few 'don'ts'; but he has few or no positive moral directives within him" (Peck and Havighurst, 1960, p. 98). Comparison with the *Taxonomy* categories suggests that such an individual has achieved beyond the first level of 1.0 *Receiving,* since the "don'ts" have differentiated the characteristics of the situation so that he can respond to them. His conformity to avoid punishment or disapproval suggests the first level of the 2.0 *Responding* category, 2.1 *Acquiescence in responding.* In fact, in defining this category, the terms "obedience" and "compliance" are used to describe this behavior.

Peck and Havighurst's next higher level is the conforming type. They describe this type as a child who "...goes along passively with the social and moral rules in a rather literal way. His acceptance is positive, if mild, for he has more liking than resentment in his general world outlook" (1960, pp. 98–99). "He follows a system of literal rules, specific for each occasion, with no overall consistency as to the degree of morality in different situations.... In a sense such a person might be said to have a crude conscience..." (1960, pp. 5–6). It is not entirely clear how much farther up the *Taxonomy* this character type carries us. Since the child is now voluntarily conforming, there is apparently a "willingness to respond," as denoted by the idea of living by the rules. The second category of the 2.0 *Responding* level, 2.2 *Willingness to respond,* seems to fit the description of the type pretty well. The next higher level, 2.3 *Satisfaction in response,* includes in its definition that the behavior be accompanied by an emotional response, possibly of pleasure or enjoyment. Although this level might be involved in describing the conforming types, since it is clear that the response is a mild one, this is not the zestful embrace of a positive value which is usually the goal the teacher envisions for this category.

The fourth type is termed irrational-conscientious; it is perceived by Peck and Havighurst as about at the same level of psychosocial maturity as the conforming type and is an alternative route through this stage of behavior. The irrational-conscientious type also lives by absolute rules but has been forced to internalize them more completely than the conformer. "If he approves of an act he sees as honest, he carries it out whether or not the people around him approve. He appeals to an abstract principle of honesty.... The irrational component is visible in the individual's customary rigidity in applying a preconceived principle.... This is 'blind' rigid superego at work" (1960, p. 7). The largely negative aspects of this type warn us that this is a stage which may not fit well in the *Taxonomy* levels. We do not often find this level specified in teachers' objectives. Perhaps this is an unrealistic omission since there is in this type an element of willingness to "stand up and be counted" in the face of social pressure which, when found in an otherwise internally consistent individual, we admire. While internal consistency is lacking at this stage, it can be conceived as a step upward toward the next level of maturity. Thus the stages of internalization described previously for the conformer would apply here, and we may find ourselves pushed a bit higher on the *Taxonomy*. Objectives describing this behavior would be classified as 3.3 *Commitment* since the student would be behaving in such a way as to demonstrate that he held a particular value.

The final type described by Peck and Havighurst is the rational-altruistic, perceived as the highest level of moral maturity. The superego of such a person "is intermingled and integrated with principles derived from rational assessment of experience.... He is actively *for* his principles, neither a passive conformist nor an intolerant 'reformer.'... He reacts with emotion appropriate to the occasion. This does not mean he is unemotional, for he is enthusiastic about promoting what is good, and aroused to prevent what is bad" (1960, pp. 100–101). Comparing this abstract of the type's description with the *Taxonomy* categories, it is clear that such individuals have achieved at the level 2.3 *Satisfaction in response* and have also achieved at the third level 3.0 *Valuing* in which the "learner displays [the] behavior with sufficient consistency in appropriate situations that he comes to be perceived as holding a value." (Part II, p. 139.) At the higher levels of *Valuing* he behaves so as to further this impression actively, a description quite consistent with the rational-altruistic type.

The next higher level of the *Taxonomy*, 4.0 *Organization*, is intended to include objectives describing the building of a system of values. It includes the stages at which the value is conceptualized and at which it is integrated into a system. Comparison of the description of the rational-altruistic stage with the *Taxonomy* indicates further congruence, for at this stage the individual "is 'rational' because he assesses each new action and its effects realistically, in the light of internalized moral principles derived from social experience" (Peck and Havighurst, 1960, p. 8).

The *Taxonomy* recognizes the changing and continuously maturing nature of the character ascribed to the rational-altruist. It describes 4.2 *Organization of a value system* as "a kind of dynamic equilibrium which is, in part, dependent upon those portions of the environment which are "salient at any point in time" (p. 159).

The highest level of the *Taxonomy* is 5.0 *Characterization by a value* or *value complex* and includes the categories 5.1 *Generalized set* and 5.2 *Characterization.* Persons at this level are pervasively controlled by an organized and integrated philosophy of life. Thus the major aspects of this category are embodied in the description of the rational-altruist. But there is an element of difference between the *Taxonomy's* top category and that of the Peck and Havighurst stages. The *Taxonomy* is designed to be neutral with respect to educational philosophies and value systems. The Peck-Havighurst rational-altruist, however, as the name implies, is "altruistic because he is ultimately interested in the welfare of others, as well as himself" (1960, p. 8). Such a description would probably be consistent with the objectives we would classify in the *Taxonomy* from schools in our culture, but it specifies a positive value direction not built into the *Taxonomy.*

The Peck-Havighurst stages stop short of the point at which the superego or conscience operates so routinely that the process is largely an unconscious one. In their rational-altruistic description they indicate that the subject "objectively assesses the results of a given act... and approves it on the grounds of whether or not it serves others as well as himself. (He may do this either consciously or unconsciously; the issue is not consciousness, but the quality of the judgment)" (1960, p. 8). Though they acknowledge at this point that the process may be unconscious, most of their description is of a conscious act ("he objectively assesses," "he sees implications," "he wants to work constructively," "his behavior is rationally oriented," etc.).

Behavior at the top level of the *Taxonomy* is perceived to be so deeply internalized that it is a habit. While this may not appear as an important difference between the Peck and Havighurst stages and the *Taxonomy,* it serves to illustrate one purpose the *Taxonomy* should serve; namely, that of providing a model or

"Mendeleyev Table" against which to test such formulations as this one. Important discrepancies would suggest that either the theoretical formulation, the *Taxonomy*, or both are in need of rethinking and possible modification.

In summary, all the relevant developmental stages of the Peck and Havighurst formulation seem to find an appropriate sequential counterpart in the *Taxonomy*. Peck and Havighurst indicate that their formulation is consistent with their research data but is based heavily on Freud. It embodies Piaget's work in its description of "the movements from adult restraint through the 'moral realism' of uncritical conformity to external rules, to an autonomous morality based upon cooperation among individuals who separately examine and rationally validate their own moral decision" (Peck and Havighurst, 1960, p. 10). Thus the *Taxonomy* framework, built around the principle of internalization and developed in such a way as to facilitate the meaningful categorization of teachers' objectives, is found to be consistent with a work having both empirical and theoretical bases.

The Neutrality of the Taxonomy

The reader may have noted in the preceding section that whereas the *Taxonomy* was perceived as "neutral," the Peck-Havighurst types embody a particular philosophy. Perhaps a word of explanation of what is meant by "neutrality" is relevant. "Neutrality" in this instance means that the taxonomic scheme should be broad enough to include objectives from any philosophic orientation, and thus from any culture. It is not yet clear that it actually is that broad since it was built and tested with products of our own culture, and all the illustrations have come from our schools. It seems unlikely that the publicly avowed objectives of most schools, in Western society, would differ markedly from ours even where the political orientation is markedly more authoritarian. On the other hand, the scheme does provide levels for the extreme inculcation of a prescribed set of values if this is the philosophy of a culture. Similarly it would appear that certain other emphases of particular cultures could also be provided for within the *Taxonomy's* scheme (e.g., an emphasis on the avoidance of any display of competition, a characteristic of at least one American Indian culture). It is to be hoped, therefore, that the scheme will prove to be neutral with respect to such orientations by its ability to include all of them within the rubrics used.

Summary

An analysis of the objectives of the affective domain showed that each included a range of meanings as they are typically used. The analysis suggested that the concept "internalization" described well the major process of the affective domain. As internalization progresses, the learner comes to attend to phenomena, to respond to them, to value them, and to conceptualize them. He organizes his values in a value complex which comes to characterize his way of life. Internalization is seen as related to socialization but is not a synonym for it. The stages of the affective domain are seen as consistent with an empirically and theoretically based point of view on conscience or superego development.

CHAPTER 4

THE RELATION OF THE AFFECTIVE TO THE COGNITIVE DOMAIN

There has been much research on and logical analysis of the relation of cognitive to affective behavior, particularly the attainment of affective goals by cognitive means. We hope that the development of the *Affective Domain Taxonomy* will stimulate further research and thought on the relation between it and the cognitive domain.

As a start in this direction some of these relationships are examined in this chapter. The initial section of the chapter examines the unity of cognitive and affective behavior. The arbitrary analytical nature of any classification scheme is noted next, as well as the fact that fragmenting analysis is fundamental to such schemes. The basic problem is how to choose an appropriate framework. The section following explores the relation between the two domains as they have been structured in the *Taxonomy*. This section is speculative and it is in need of empirical test. In the succeeding section, the relation between cognitive and affective behavior is studied in the way one domain is used as a means of controlling behavior and achieving objectives in the other. Finally, in the last section, certain differences between the domains that are of particular importance in school teaching and testing are discussed.

The Fundamental Unity of the Organism

The fact that we attempt to analyze the affective area separately from the cognitive is not intended to suggest that there is a fundamental separation. There is none. As Scheerer puts it, "...behavior may be conceptualized as being embedded in a cognitive-emotional-motivational matrix in which no true separation is possible. No matter how we slice behavior, the ingredients of motivation-emotion-cognition are present in one order or another" (Scheerer, 1954, p. 123).

Scheerer's point is well taken; yet to conceptualize behavior adequately we must tease it apart into components of some kind, all the while keeping in mind the interrelation of these components. Thus note how William James, writing in 1890 and using the term "subjective" in place of "affective," initially recognizes the unity of the two domains but then analytically proceeds to explain how cognitive behavior is involved in affective behavior:

> The contrast is not, then ... between certain subjective facts called images and sensations and others called acts of relating intelligence. ... The contrast is really between two aspects, in which all mental facts without exception may be taken; their structural aspect, as being subjective, and their functional aspect, as being cognitions. In the former aspect, the highest as well as the lowest is a feeling. ... In the latter aspect, the lowest mental fact as well as the highest may grasp some bit of truth as its content. ... From the cognitive point of view, all mental facts are intellections. From the subjective point of view, all are feelings. ...
>
> And then we see that the current opposition of Feeling to Knowledge is quite a false issue. If every feeling is at the same time a bit of knowledge, we ought no longer to talk of mental states differing by having more or less of the cognitive quality; they only differ in knowing more or less, in having much fact or little fact for their object. The feeling of a broad scheme of relations is a feeling that knows much; the feeling of a simple quality is a feeling that knows little.[1]

Similarly, Rokeach points out that in analyzing cognitive behavior he is at the same time working with affective states, for every cognitive behavior has its affective counterpart:

> ...analysis in terms of beliefs and systems of beliefs does not necessarily restrict us only to the study of cognitive behavior. We assume that every affective state also has its representation as a cognitive state in the form of some belief or some structural relation among beliefs within a system. With respect to the enjoyment of music, for example, we all build up through past experience a set of beliefs or expectancies about what constitutes "good" and "bad" music. It is in terms of such expectancies, which are more often implicit than explicit, that we enjoy a particular composition. Thus, a person who is exposed to a particular piece of classical music or jazz may enjoy it, even though it may be totally unfamiliar to him, because it is congruent with an already existing set of beliefs he has built up over time. Depending on the extent to which he is prepared to entertain new systems, he may or may not enjoy Schönberg or other music perceived as incompatible with his own beliefs about what constitutes good music. ... In all cases, enjoyment or its opposite is the affective counterpart of a belief organization and can be thought of as being in one-to-one relation (isomorphic) with it. Thus, our cognitive approach is as much concerned with affection as with cognition.[2]

---

[1] James, 1890, pp. 478–79.

[2] Rokeach, 1960, p. 399.

Thus James, a forerunner of modern psychology, admits a fundamental unity of affective and cognitive behavior but proceeds to a fragmenting analysis showing how one is involved in the other. That this kind of reasoning continues is indicated by Rokeach, a contempory psychologist who, also realizing the unity, shows how the one domain is involved in the other. This is what we, too, have done in developing the *Taxonomy.* Our problem has been (recognizing the arbitrariness of our conceptualization) to gain a perspective of our task essential to the formulating of a useful framework.

The Arbitrariness of Classification Schemes

Every classification scheme is an abstraction which arbitrarily makes divisions among phenomena solely for the convenience of the user, more particularly to emphasize some special characteristic of the phenomena of importance to the user. Some of these divisions seem "natural," since they correspond to differences which are readily perceived in the phenomena categorized. In other instances, the differences may be much more difficult to perceive and thus seem more arbitrary. One may find both "natural" and quite arbitrary classifications within the same framework, depending upon the nature of the phenomenon to be classified and what is important to the person using the framework. To the biochemist, the dichotomy between the physical and the biological sciences is extremely arbitrary, and there is nothing "natural" about it, though this division may be highly useful and "natural" to the administrators of a large university.

The arbitrariness of the *Taxonomy* structure is at once apparent in, among other things,[3] its division of the realm of educational goals into three domains: cognitive, affective, and psychomotor. These seem to be "natural" divisions, since teachers and educators have more or less traditionally divided their objectives into these categories, either explicitly or implicitly. It is hoped that the divisions within each of the domains will also seem "natural," once the reader is familiar with them. We have tried to make the

[3]We could, for example, cite as arbitrary the insistence that educational goals are most meaningfully stated as student behaviors rather than teacher activities. But this aspect is less relevant to the chapter topic.

breaks between categories at what appeared to be the "natural" places without attempting to force a correspondence between domains. Whether this permits the most useful and meaningful analysis remains for the user to judge. We have already, in Chapter 2, shown the need for a classification structure and given an indication of how it is hoped the *Taxonomy* can usefully and meaningfully fill that need. The increasing use of the *Taxonomy's* already published portion encourages us to believe that this kind of analysis has proved useful and meaningful and that this second portion may prove to be of worth as well.

With full recognition of the arbitrariness of the *Taxonomy's* division between cognitive and affective behavior, we may find it helpful to examine the way teachers' statements of objectives split cognitive from affective behavior, and then how the cognitive domain is related to the affective in terms of the particular categories used in this taxonomic analysis.

The Affective Component of Cognitive Objectives

The "garden variety" of objectives concentrates on specifying behavior in only one domain at a time. No doubt this results from the customarily analytic approaches to building curricula. Only occasionally do we find a statement like "The student should learn to analyze a good argument with pleasure." Such a statement suggests not only the cognitive behavior but also the affective aspect that accompanies it. In spite of the lack of explicit formulation, however, nearly all cognitive objectives have an affective component if we search for it. Most instructors hope that their students will develop a continuing interest in the subject matter taught. They hope that their students will have learned certain attitudes toward the phenomena dealt with or toward the way in which problems are approached. But they leave these goals unspecified. This means that many of the objectives which are classified in the cognitive domain have an implicit but unspecified affective component that could be concurrently classified in the affective domain. Where such an attitude or interest objective refers, as it most often does, to the content of the course as a whole or at least to a sizable segment of it, it may be most convenient to specify it as a separate objective. Many such affective objectives—the interest objective, for example—become the affective components of all or most of the cognitive objectives in the course. The affective domain is useful in emphasizing the fact that affective components exist and in analyzing their nature. Perhaps by its very existence it will encourage greater development of affective components of cognitive objectives.

It is possible that a different affective objective accompanies every cognitive objective in a course.[4] Were this a common situation, the present form of the *Taxonomy* would be unwieldy, for it would require a dual categorization of each objective. While the present state of the art of curriculum development suggests that the latter concern is by no means immediate, this is not a possibility to be discarded.

The relation of cognitive to affective objectives as conceived by teachers is mirrored in the relations of the taxonomies of the two domains. We turn next to this matter.

Relations between the Taxonomy Categories of the Two Domains

When one looks for relations between the subcategories of the two domains one finds that they clearly overlap. This overlap is implicit in the following descriptions of roughly parallel steps in the two continua. The terms set in italic are used as heads of divisions in the *Taxonomy* of the cognitive or affective domains. Their category numbers are given in parentheses. (Appendixes A and B may be helpful to the reader in providing summaries of the two continua.)

1. The cognitive continuum begins with the student's recall and recognition of *Knowledge* (1.0),	1. The affective continuum begins with the student's merely *Receiving* (1.0) stimuli and passively attending to it. It extends through his more actively attending to it,
2. it extends through his *Comprehension* (2.0) of the knowledge,	2. his *Responding* (2.0) to stimuli on request, willingly responding to these stimuli, and taking satisfaction in this responding,

Cont. on next pg.

[4]This is not to imply that the full range from 1.1 to 5.2 of affective behaviors would apply to every cognitive objective, however. This matter is explored further in the next section in this chapter.

3. his skill in *Application* (3.0) of the knowledge that he comprehends,

4. his skill in *Analysis* (4.0) of situations involving this knowledge, his skill in *Synthesis* (5.0) of this knowledge into new organizations,

5. his skill in *Evaluation* (6.0) in that area of knowledge to judge the value of material and methods for given purposes.

3. his *Valuing* (3.0) the phenomenon or activity so that he voluntarily responds and seeks out ways to respond,

4. his *Conceptualization* (4.1) of each value responded to,

5. his *Organization* (4.2) of these values into systems and finally organizing the value complex into a single whole, a *Characterization* (5.0) of the individual.

The most apparent places at which the affective domain meets the cognitive domain in this description are at steps 1, 4, and 5. Setting the two domains parallel, as we have done to facilitate the examination of the relationship, suggests a much closer level-to-level correspondence than actually exists, however. Let us examine this correspondence, taking steps 1, 4, and 5, and 2 and 3 in that order.

Step 1. The first point of close parallelism between the domains is at step 1, where "receiving" a phenomenon, or attending to it to some extent, corresponds to having "knowledge" of the phenomenon. But the emphasis in 1.0 *Receiving* is different from that in 1.0 *Knowledge* in that we are less concerned with memory and retrieval on demand. There is a relation, however, for certainly attending to a phenomenon is prerequisite to knowing about it. Further, only as one is willing to attend to a phenomenon will he learn about it.

On first glance, one might assume that "receiving" would always refer to awareness of certain information, and thus its parallel in the cognitive domain would always be the *Knowledge* category (e.g., the simple awareness of the way perspective is portrayed in a painting). While frequently true, this is not necessarily the case. Thus, *Receiving* includes the objective "Listens to music with some discrimination as to its mood and meaning and with some recognition of the contributions of various musical elements and instruments to the total effect." This certainly involves 2.0 *Comprehension,* the second category of the cognitive continuum, and probably 3.0 *Application* and 4.0 *Analysis,* the third and fourth levels of it. On looking over the objectives in the lowest levels of the affective domain, however, this is about as high a level in the cognitive continuum as one finds implied by the cognitive concomitants of these affective objectives.

But whatever the behavior specified in the lowest level in the affective domain, it is almost a certainty that one could interpret the objective so that, except for the fact that it is a building stone for more complex affective objectives, the objective might be restated so as to be classified in the cognitive domain. Some of our critics have argued that we should have begun the affective domain with 2.0 *Responding,* because of the heavily cognitive nature of this bottom category. But the fact that this behavior is a necessary first step to building objectives higher in the affective-domain hierarchy is the reason—an important one—for its being included as the bottom rung in the affective domain. Further, the emphasis in "receiving" is different from that of "knowledge," stressing, as is proper for an affective category, the volitional aspects of the knowing act.

Steps 4 and 5. A second point of apparent close contact between the affective and cognitive domains is the correspondence in the upper levels of the two continua at steps 4 and 5. Here the behavior described by the affective domain is at least in part cognitive, as the student conceptualizes a value to which he has been responding, and this value is in turn integrated and organized into a system of values which comes eventually to characterize the individual. Such objectives would appear to require, at the very least, the ability to 2.0 *Comprehend,* for the student must translate his behavior into a set of verbal terms describing the value involved. In some instances this might call for the student to 4.0 *Analyze* the common value element from a series of activities or situations in which he has been involved and to 5.0 *Synthesize* this commonality into a value which encompasses all of them. The ability to organize and interrelate values into systems must certainly call for the ability to 4.0 *Analyze,* as it is described in the cognitive domain, and the development of new value complexes also most likely involves the ability to 5.0 *Synthesize.* Further, the ability to balance values against one another, which is implied by the very highest affective categories, implies capability for 6.0 *Evalutaion* as it is defined in the cognitive domain. For example, "Judges problems and issues in terms of situations, issues, purposes, and consequences involved rather than in terms of fixed, dogmatic precepts or emotionally wishful thinking" (Part II, p. 184).

It is possible, however, that in everyday behavior much of this balancing of values is at a semiconscious intuitive level rather than at the rational, objective, conscious, level implied by 6.0 *Evaluation* in the cognitive domain. Such semiconscious behavior is described in the affective domain by category 5.1 *Generalized Set,* where the behavior is so internalized that it is displayed almost automatically, without conscious consideration. On the surface, this makes the affective domain appear to extend further than the cognitive in the sense that it describes a behavior so deeply internalized that it is automatic. No such behavior appears in the cognitive continuum.

But one could argue that some cognitive evaluation behavior ought also to be that well learned. Indeed, one may question whether such regularity of behavior is not implicit in most cognitive and affective objectives at all *Taxonomy* levels. In general, in both the cognitive and affective domains the regularity of behavior is measured, not in terms of the *Taxonomy* level of behavior, but as such regularity affects the test score. Given a test which includes a variety of situations in which the observed behavior should be displayed if learned or internalized, the regularity with which it is displayed across these situations is reflected in the person's score. At the top level of the affective domain we happen to have specified a level of behavior which is so well learned, so deeply internalized, that it is automatic.

In this sense, at the 5.1 *Generalized Set* level we have described a kind of behavior which can be attained only with complete regularity, and the level of performance required in scoring is implicit in the behavior description. (This is the only category in the *Taxonomy* which so specifies the score performance for achievement of that level.) It was included because affective objectives were found which described this regularity of the behavior. Certain affective objectives have made explicit a complete regularity and automaticity of response which may also be implied in many cognitive objectives. Thus a discrepancy wherein the affective domain appears to extend beyond the cognitive domain can be reconciled on careful examination. The overlap between the two domains at this level appears to be real.

Steps 2 and 3. In the middle portions of the affective continuum the individual begins to respond to the stimuli, at first on request (2.1 *Acquiescence in responding*), then increasingly on his own volition to the point where he is actively seeking instances in which he may respond (3.3 *Commitment*). These are not unrelated to the cognitive domain, but the nature of the relation is much less easily specified. The range of cognitive behavior corresponding to this portion of the affective continuum appears to cover a wide portion of the cognitive domain. But in all the affective behavior the cognitive element is present and implied. For example, in the lowest level of this portion, in the subcategory 2.1 *Acquiescence in responding*, we find the objective "Willingness to comply with health regulations." This objective implies that at least there is comprehension of these regulations and the ability to apply them to new situations; both of these are cognitive behaviors. At the highest level of this middle range of the continuum, in the subcategory 3.3 *Commitment,* we find the objective "Devotion to those ideas and ideals which are the foundation of democracy." This objective in turn implies cognitive behaviors such as the ability to analyze situations in order to determine how the ideas and ideals apply in a given situation.

It can be noted that throughout this analysis of the five steps there is some tendency for the cognitive counterpart of a low-level objective to come from the lower levels of the affective continuum and for objectives at the upper level of the affective continuum to have upper-level cognitive counterparts.

From the analysis above, it appears that at all levels of the affective domain, affective objectives have a cognitive component, and one can find affective components for cognitive objectives. But lest this relationship appear more obvious than it really is, it should be noted that the examples of objectives in the preceding discussion were chosen so as to make the relation clear. We could have chosen affective-domain objectives for which the cognitive component is much more obscure; for instance, "Enjoyment of worship" or "Responds emotionally to a work of art." While we could recognize a cognitive component in such objectives, we should clearly be less certain to secure agreement among educators about the most appropriate cognitive behavior to accompany the affective behavior. Though undoubtedly there is some cognitive component in every affective objective, its nature is much more easily seen in some instances than in others.

Other Relationships between the Cognitive and Affective Domains

Some of the more interesting relationships between the cognitive and affective domains (and some of the clearer indications of the interrelatedness of the two domains) are those in which the attainment of a goal or objective of one domain is viewed as the means to the attainment of a goal or objective in the other. In some instances we use changes in the cognitive domain as a means to make changes in the affective; e.g., we give the student information intended to change his attitude. In other instances we use an affective goal as a means to achieve a cognitive one; e.g., we develop an interest in material so the student will learn to use it.

Let us examine these two situations, as well as the instance where we seek affective and cognitive goals simultaneously. Finally, let us note some differences between the two domains that are important for teaching and testing in the school situation.

Cognitive Objectives as Means to Affective Goals

The fact that our learning research and theories focus largely on cognitive behavior is an indication that we feel we know better how to handle the cognitive domain. Moving from the cognitive domain to the affective thus tends to be the preferred orientation. Attitudes, and even feelings, for example, tend to be defined in cognitive terms. James, in the quotation cited earlier in this chapter, defined feeling as a kind of knowing. Asch (1952) stated that an "attitude contains a more or less coherent ordering of data... an organization of experience and data with reference to an object" (p. 580). Rhine (1958) surveyed the definitions of attitudes by outstanding psychologists and concluded that the common element is the essence of what is generally meant by a concept. He therefore defined an attitude as a concept with an evaluative component and proceeded to explain attitude formation in the cognitive terms usually reserved for concept formation. As he pointed out, this approach could make attitudes more amenable to laboratory scrutiny, one indication of why this approach to the affective domain is preferred.

Rokeach, as already noted, saw a basic congruence between the cognitive and affective systems. He stated further, "...although our approach to belief systems, including esthetic ones, is a purely cognitive one... if the assumption is correct that every emotion has its cognitive counterpart, then we should be able to reach down into the complexities of man's emotional life via a study of his cognitive processes. . . . If we know something about the way a person relates himself to the world of ideas we may also be able to say in what way he relates himself to the world of people and to authority" (Rokeach, 1960, p.8).

Similarly, Rosenberg (1956) examined attitudes in terms of cognitive structure. Noting the relations between cognitive and affective components, he argued that a tendency to respond to an object with positive or negative affect is "accompanied by a cognitive structure made up of beliefs about the potentialities of that object for attaining or blocking the realization of valued states" (p. 367). He further argued that both the direction of the affect—whether it is positive or negative with reference to the object—and the strength of the affect are correlated with the content of the associated cognitive structure. Here again we see the affective component made a function of cognitive components which are more easily dealt with, thus permitting manipulation of the affective by the cognitive.

Festinger (1957) and Heider (1958), among others, have propounded so-called "balance theories" which provide another approach to the study of affective changes as a result of cognitive behavior. Festinger, in his theory of cognitive dissonance, described the motivating effect of disharmonious or dissonant states in cognition. He defined cognition so broadly as to include affectively tinged states such as opinions and beliefs as well as cognitive states of knowledge. Thus his theory easily bridges the cognitive-affective distinction and cannot be seen as one which manipulates cognitive behavior (in its usual sense) alone. But Festinger did describe the effects of changes in knowledge on affective behavior, and this represents one kind of approach to affective behavior through cognition.

The careful observer of the classroom can see that the wise teacher as well as the psychological theorist uses cognitive behavior and the achievement of cognitive goals to attain affective goals. In many instances she does so more intuitively than consciously. In fact, a large part of what we call "good teaching" is the teacher's ability to attain affective objectives through challenging the students' fixed beliefs and getting them to discuss issues.

In some instances teachers use cognitive behavior not just as a means to affective behavior but as a kind of prerequisite. Thus appreciation objectives are often approached cognitively by having the student analyze a work of art so that he will come to understand the way in which certain effects are produced—the nuances of shading to produce depth, color to produce emotional tone, etc. Such analysis on a cognitive level, when mastered, may be seen as learning necessary for "truly" appreciating a work of art.

In other instances teachers use cognitive behavior and cognitive goals as a means to multiple affective ends. This occurs especially in areas where the problem of indoctrination arises. Cognitive behavior may be used to indoctrinate points of view and to build attitudes and values. Indeed, we do this shamelessly in the aesthetic fields, where we want our students to learn to recognize "good" poetry, painting, architecture, sculpture, music, and so on. But in most areas of the curriculum we have a horror of indoctrinating the student with any but our most basic core values (we cannot always agree on the nature of these core values, the court cases on religion in the schools are an example). In most instances where indoctrination is avoided, we seek to have the student take his own position with respect to the issue. Thus a discussion may result in the development of a variety of "correct" positions and attitudes with respect to the area of concern, rather than in a single type of behavioral outcome as when a cognitive objective has been achieved. This also occurs where there are conflicts in values within our own culture. For example, the problems of honesty vs. dishonesty vs. "white lies," or of competition vs. cooperation, usually result in a variety of acceptable solutions, each a function of the situation in which such a conflict arises.

There are some instances where the cognitive route to affective achievement has resulted in learning just the opposite of that intended. Thus the infamous example of the careful and detailed study of "good" English classics, which was intended to imbue us with a love of deathless prose, has in many instances alienated us from it instead. Emphasis on very high mastery of one domain may in some instances be gained at the expense of the other.

Similarly, as noted in Chapter 2, emphasis on one domain may tend to drive out the other. New courses often start with a careful analysis of both cognitive and affective objectives. But we feel more comfortable in teaching for cognitive than for affective objectives. Our drive for subject-matter mastery and the ever-increasing amount of knowledge available gives us more and more subject matter to cover. Further, our preference for approaching affective achievement through the attainment of cognitive objectives tends to focus attention on these cognitive goals as ends in themselves without our determining whether they are actually serving as means to an affective end. Over time the emphasis in most courses tends more and more to concentrate on the cognitive objectives at the expense of the affective ones. This erosion may be inevitable, but it could be lessened or stopped if we were conscious of its action. One of the major uses of *Handbook I: Cognitive Domain* has been to provide a basis for showing the current overwhelming emphasis on knowledge objectives at the expense of the development of skills and abilities in using that knowledge. Similarly, the development of *Handbook II: Affective Domain* should help to highlight the current emphasis on cognitive objectives at the expense of the affective.

Affective Objectives as Means to Cognitive Goals

From the previous discussion it seems clear that the cognitive approach to affective objectives is a frequently traveled route. What about the reverse? One of the main kinds of affective-domain objectives which are sought as means to cognitive ends is the development of interest or motivation. As viewed from the cognitive pole, the student may be treated as an analytic machine, a "computer" that solves problems. In contrast, viewed from the affective pole, we take greater cognizance of the motivation, drives, and emotions that are the factors bringing about achievement of cognitive behavior.

Obviously motivation is critical to learning and thus is one of the major ways in which the affective domain is used as a means to the cognitive. The large number of interest objectives indicates the importance of this aspect of the learning situation. The influence of hedonic tone on memory and learning is also important: children are more likely to learn and remember material for which they have a positive feeling.[5] Note for instance the prevalence of girls who dislike mathematics and so cannot learn it, as well as boys who dislike school in general and do poorly.

[5]See also the discussion of preference effects on perception in 1.0 *Receiving* (pp. 98–99).

Though these "likes" may be produced by role expectancies, it is the internalized preferences which produce the effect.

Where educational objectives are involved we are almost always concerned with positive affect, with leading rather than driving the student into learning. But there are some school situations where negative affect is used to prevent certain behaviors from occurring and to facilitate cognitive learning. Such is the use of negative affect (fear of punishment, for instance) rather than the attempt to attain affective objectives as means to cognitive ends. In some instances social pressure may be exerted to change a student's position or viewpoint. We recognized that occasionally the school will have affective goals of this kind when we provided category 2.1 *Acquiescence in responding* but noted that this was a rarely used category.

Both the theoretical and experimental literature suggest that this is not an easy route to cognitive change. Both Kelman's (1958) model, discussed in Chapter 3, and Jahoda (1956) point to the likelihood that persons may outwardly comply under such situations but inwardly remain unchanged. Festinger's (1957) theory of cognitive dissonance posits that severe external threat or pressure represents a justification to the individual for engaging in behavior contrary to his beliefs, so that there is less need to reduce the dissonance caused by his engaging in this behavior under the threat conditions. Where the threat is mild, there is less justification for engaging in the behavior, and we can thus expect more change in private opinion to reduce the dissonance. Experimentation by Festinger and Carlsmith (1959) backs up this theoretical prediction. It appears that certain threatening school climates could actually defeat teachers' attempts to bring about both cognitive and affective learning.

But, as already noted, more often our motivation results from positive affect. Increasingly this is taking the form of building upon the method of self-discovery as a means of fostering interest in learning material. In thus enhancing curiosity and exploratory activity we may be building upon a basic drive. White (1959), giving careful consideration to previous literature on motivation and to recent experimentation on curiosity and the attractiveness of novel stimuli, posits a drive for competency, a need for a feeling of efficacy. He suggests that curiosity, exploratory behavior, manipulation, and general activity bring man in contact with his environment and make him more competent to deal with it.

White's competency drive underlies these and similar activities. Few of us have recognized that with discovery-type objectives we may have been building on a basic drive.

Discovery-type material, such as that going into the University of Illinois School Mathematics Program, uses the affective effects of self-discovery as a means of simultaneously achieving the goals of mastery of the material and developing interest in it (see also Chapter 6, pages 85–86). This corresponds to what Bruner (1960) points to as an important goal in our new curricula. He suggests that we must increase "the inherent interest of the materials taught, giving the student a sense of discovery, translating what we say into thought forms appropriate to the child and so on. What this amounts to is developing in the child an interest in what he is learning and with it an appropriate set of attitudes and values about intellectual activities in general" (p. 73). This suggestion, that we build in a set of attitudes toward learning and the value of learning, represents another of the all-encompassing goals of most curricula. It is another common way in which attainment of the affective goal is a means to the facilitation of cognitive learning.

Simultaneous Achievement of Cognitive and Affective Goals

In some instances it is impossible to tell whether the affective goal is being used as a means to a cognitive goal or vice versa. It is a chicken and egg proposition. Perhaps it is fairest to say they are both being sought simultaneously.

Suchman's inquiry training appears to illustrate this and also seems a means to the goal suggested by Bruner in the quotation above. Suchman (1962) simultaneously achieves the affective goal of interest in the material through discovery learning and of building attitudes toward intellectual activity (as well as skill in it) through developing the child's inquiry ability. He uses a method analogous to the game of "Twenty Questions." As the children ask questions about an experiment shown them on film, seeking to arrive at an explanation of the puzzling phenomenon they have seen, the instructor plays the role solely of a data giver. He observes the pattern of their strategy and critiques it after a period of questioning. Thus the instructor achieves cognitive goals of improving the skill of inquiring; he does so in a self-discovery situation with a puzzling phenomenon that produces an interest in the child; by critiquing the strategy he builds an enduring motivation to use successful inquiry skill which should give support to this new-found ability in other situations.

Suchman's initial study showed marked changes in skill in questioning, but the transfer of the inquiry method to new situations showed no difference between control and experimental groups. Unfortunately Suchman did not evaluate any of the affective outcomes of his method, though he notes that it had a "marked effect on the motivation, autonomy and question asking fluency of children" (p. 126).

In some instances the joint seeking of affective and cognitive goals results in curricula which use one domain as the means to the other on a closely-knit alternating basis. Thus a cognitive skill is built and then used in rewarding situations so that affective interest in the task is built up to permit the next cognitive task to be achieved, and so on. Perhaps it is analogous to a man scaling a wall using two step ladders side by side, each with rungs too wide apart to be conveniently reached in a single step. One ladder represents the cognitive behaviors and objectives, the other the affective. The ladders are so constructed that the rungs of one ladder fall between the rungs of the other. The attainment of some complex goal is made possible by alternately climbing a rung on one ladder, which brings the next rung of the other ladder within reach. Thus alternating between affective and cognitive domains, one may seek a cognitive goal using the attainment of a cognitive goal to raise interest (an affective goal). This permits achievement of a higher cognitive goal, and so on.

Some School-Related Differences between the Cognitive and Affective Domains

In the cognitive domain we are concerned that the student shall be able to do a task when requested. In the affective domain we are more concerned that he *does do* it when it is appropriate after he has learned that he *can do* it. Even though the whole school system rewards the student more on a *can do* than on a *does do* basis, it is the latter which every instructor seeks. By emphasizing this aspect of the affective components, the affective domain brings to light an extremely important and often missing element in cognitive objectives.

Because of the emphasis on *does do* behavior in the affective domain, evaluation of achievement is more difficult. In many instances producing the "right" answer is not so much a matter of ability or of previous learning. It is more often a matter of perceiving that a behavior which is already in the student's repertoire is appropriate and expected at a given point in time. When behavior is produced solely as a result of this perception of expectancy on the part of an authority figure, it is difficult to evaluate the levels of the affective continuum above 2.1 *Acquiescence in responding*. Removal of clues that the behavior is being observed in the school setting, concealed observation in a more realistic nonschool setting (e.g., the playground), elimination of the authority aspect of the situation by assuring anonymity or by assuring that the behavior will not be graded—these are the major means used to elicit *does do* behavior and evaluate the achievement of *does do* objectives.

Another difference in evaluation between the cognitive and affective domains is the difficulty of applying standards. We have already referred to this in the previous discussion of indoctrination. While there may be only one "right" kind of achievement for an objective in the cognitive domain, there may be many "right" behaviors equally correct in achieving an objective in the affective domain.

With some affective objectives the "right" answer can be judged only in terms of the criteria which the student sets for himself (e.g., realistically setting one's own limitations and accepting these limits). This requires obtaining a record of covert process to determine achievement. Process is difficult enough to record in the cognitive domain where it can be brought to consciousness. In the affective domain where feelings as well as thoughts mediate, it is still more difficult. Further, our respect for the private views of individuals prevents our asking certain kinds of questions. The reward our culture places on "keeping our feelings to ourselves" makes observations of emotional responses more difficult; this is truer with the older, acculturated, and socialized youth than with the child. The low validities of both self-report and projective tests suggest that the inference problem has yet to be solved. Thus testing for affective achievement where the "right" answer depends on this kind of inference is as yet most difficult to do.

Summary

This chapter really only scratches the surface of what is undoubtedly a very complex relationship between the cognitive and affective domains. We still have much to learn about it. But the fact should be clear that the two domains are tightly intertwined. Each affective behavior has a cognitive-behavior counterpart of some kind and vice versa. An objective in one domain has a counterpart in the opposite domain, though often we do not take cognizance of it. There is some correlation between the *Taxonomy* levels of an affective objective and its cognitive counterpart. Each domain is sometimes used as a means to the other, though the more common route is from the cognitive to the affective. Theory statements exist which permit us to express one in terms of the other and vice versa.

Our split between the affective and cognitive domains is for analytical purposes and is quite arbitrary. Hopefully the analysis of the two domains will have heuristic value so that we may better understand the nature of each as well as the relationship of one to the other.

CHAPTER 5

THE CLASSIFICATION OF EDUCATIONAL OBJECTIVES AND MEASURES IN THE AFFECTIVE DOMAIN

This chapter is intended to help the reader make practical use of the *Taxonomy* in classifying educational objectives and measures of these objectives. Following a brief discussion of some of the problems of classification, examples of classification and samples for the reader to classify for himself demonstrate how the *Taxonomy* can be used. The reader is given the authors' key to the samples so that he can check his mastery of the system.

Each category of the affective continuum is defined in three ways in Part II of this Handbook. First there is a verbal description of the behavior in the category. This is probably the most complete definition. We have tried to make the description as exact as possible.

A second type of definition is provided by a list of educational objectives which follows each category description. These objectives were selected from published and unpublished materials relating to actual courses or to curriculum program statements. In most instances, however, they have been modified to better express the behavior intended. The objectives were selected to represent a range of subject-matter fields.

The third definition is provided by the illustrations of measures for each category. These questions have been drawn from tests already existing, many of them originally developed during the Eight-Year Study of the Progressive Education Association. Again an effort has been made to cover a range of subject-matter fields, but it is by no means all-inclusive. The preponderance of measures is of the objective type. This does not reflect a bias against projective or free-response devices (though there is much evidence in the literature which would support such a bias), but these seemed to be the clearest evaluation examples.

In order to help the reader obtain an over-all view of the *Taxonomy* and to help in its use, a condensed version of both domains appears in the Appendix.

The Classification of Objectives

By far the biggest problem which the potential classifier will encounter in dealing with affective-domain objectives is the vagueness of the terms used in these objectives and the range of meanings which may be assumed for even the most commonly used terms. In previous sections (see especially Chapters 2 and 3) we have dealt at length with this problem. There is little point in repeating it here, except to indicate that the classifier may often have to rewrite the objective to indicate the particular interpretation which he is giving to the terms in classifying it. While this may appear to be doing violence to its original intent, this objection ceases to be valid when it is realized that as they stand these objectives give little guidance to the selection of instructional practices or to their evaluation. Until the objective is clearly specified, it can serve only to indicate broad general directions. The use of the *Taxonomy* as a means of clarifying the specific meaning intended can add greatly to the usefulness of objectives by making them more operational. It is also a way of insuring that the meaning intended by the curriculum maker is the meaning understood by test constructors, teachers, and others.

While making the objective more specific is the major problem facing the *Taxonomy* user, there are others, some of which are illustrated in the following examples. The first example is limited to a single field to highlight the way in which objectives relate to the points defined on the affective continuum. Objectives chosen from the field of art have been arranged in a hierarchical order, with the basis for classification described. Although, in practice, one would rarely find such parallel wording between levels, it was intentionally created in these objectives to illustrate the changes from level to level. In all instances it is understood that the objective is to describe the student behavior to be attained.

Develops some consciousness of the use of shading to portray depth and lighting in a picture.

At this level we are simply asking the student to be aware of the fact that shading is present in a picture and that it is used to increase the three-dimensional sense of the picture, often at the same time that it indicates the direction and brilliance of the lighting. The student is not asked to evaluate, or even necessarily to verbalize, this phenomenon, but simply to be aware of it. This objective would be classified as 1.1 *Awareness*.

Develops a tolerance for bizarre uses of shading in modern art.

This is at a slightly higher level than the preceding objective, since we assume that the student is aware of shading but may be repelled by some of its bizarre uses and by the mood that it sets. The objective merely indicates that it is hoped that he will be willing to pay some attention to shading in such pictures and not reject the picture for the way shading is used. We would thus classify this objective as 1.2 *Willingness to receive.*

Is on the alert for instances in which shading has been used to create a sense of three-dimensional depth at the same time that it indicates something about the lighting in a picture.

Here again we assume not only that the student will attend to the use of shading but that he is willing to pay attention to it when confronted with examples. He will be looking for examples of the aesthetic principles which have been discussed as a first step in art appreciation. Note that he is not yet actively seeking out such examples but is alert for them when they appear—in this case alert for the particular use of shading for double effect (dimensionality and lighting). This objective would be classified as 1.3 *Controlled or selected attention.*

Perhaps this is the place to note that all of the above would be most typically found as an objective stated as "appreciate the use of shading in a picture." In some instances it might be further qualified by the phrase "to portray depth and shading," but more often even this phrase would be omitted. By specifying three levels as is done here, one has begun to delineate the behaviors involved so that they provide more accurate guidance to the classroom teacher. She can then know how to structure the classroom activities so that these behaviors are evoked and can recognize and reward them as they appear.

Voluntarily looks for instances of good art where shading, perspective, color, and design have been well used.

This objective assumes still greater internalization on the part of the student of what constitutes "good art," as that concept has been taught in the classroom. It further assumes that the individual has accepted these as his own criteria and voluntarily uses them. We would therefore classify this as 2.2 *Willingness to respond.*

Enjoys finding instances of good art where shading, perspective, color, and design have been well used.

The word "enjoy" immediately suggests that the salient feature of this objective is the emotional component which accompanies the response. The category 2.3 *Satisfaction in response* is used for these objectives.

The reader may wonder here about the order of this and the preceding objectives. Does enjoyment precede voluntarily undertaking some action, or is it concomitant? He is referred to a fuller treatment (Part II, pages 130–31) of the problem of locating the point on the affective continuum where the emotional component of response should be placed. Suffice to say here that no one position for this subcategory on the continuum will be entirely satisfactory for all objectives. Emotion as an accompaniment of the response first appears at different points; its location at 2.3 appears to be a kind of reasonable average of such locations.

The student seeks out examples of good art for enjoyment of them.

The difference between "voluntarily looks for" and "seeks out" may be too subtle to illustrate clearly the advance over the previous level. What is intended is that at this level the individual has clearly identified "good art" as of value, and one would recognize this in the active search for examples of such art. This actively pursuing, seeking out, or wanting is a characteristic of 3.2 *Preference for a value.*

Desires to evaluate works of art which are appreciated.

The process of evaluation of a work of art involves the determination of the desirable and undesirable features of it; it means the conceptualization of these features so that the individual is aware of them. This objective would thus be categorized under 4.1 *Conceptualization of a value.*

Acceptance of the place of art in one's life as one of dominant value.

Not only is the individual committed to art as a value, but in contrast to many other possibilities he has yielded it a priority position. This means that he has begun to arrange his values into a hierarchy, to interrelate and organize them. This would be classified as 4.2 *Organization of a value system.*

Views all problems primarily in terms of their aesthetic aspects.

The individual has come to be so committed to art that the aesthetic aspects of problems are dominant; it is a routine way of looking at things, a set. This would be classified as 5.1 *Gen-*

eralized Set. It is unlikely that such an objective would be found in any curricula except for those designed for art majors, but it does illustrate the pervasive quality which is expected when objectives are classified at this level.

These examples may serve to illustrate the manner in which the objectives of a curriculum area change as they are carried to higher and higher levels in the affective continuum. In some instances, the wordings of the objectives were hardly precise enough to make clear the subtle differences which occur from category to category as the continuum is scaled. Thus, by classifying an objective we lend a precision to its statement which is difficult to obtain even with careful wording.

Not all the examples which are given in Part II have been reworded to yield maximum precision and clarity. We wanted to give the reader an idea of what commonly worded objectives might be included in the category. He will find instances of objectives that are rather grossly worded; in fact, where the same words are used in different categories. Objectives worded in this manner could be classified in the particular category if they were interpreted in the limited manner in which the category is defined. As examples of this, it was noted with respect to the sample objective classified at the 1.3 level that it and many of those classified at 1.1 and 1.2 would have been phrased typically as appreciation objectives. Some of the others, such as those classified in the second, third, and fourth levels, might have been phrased as attitudes or values in their typical form.

The reader may find it helpful to survey the range of meanings which it is possible to infer from objectives. An instance is given in Chapter 2, page 22, where an "interest" objective is examined from this standpoint.

Perhaps we will have enough illustrations if we classify an objective in need of clarification. The following objective appears in the course objectives for "American Thought and Language," a general education course at Michigan State University: *An active acceptance of the responsibility for intellectual honesty in effective communication.* In order to classify this objective, one would have to determine what is meant by "an active acceptance of...responsibility." This is clearly beyond the 1.0 *Receiving* level and below the 4.0 *Organization* level. The problem then becomes one of determining where it falls in the second and third categories. The second category, *Responding*, is indicative of a rather low level of commitment. It is more appropriate for interest- and appreciation-level objectives. "An active acceptance" implies that the individual is actively pursuing the responsibility, is acting it out. We would therefore locate this objective in the third level, *Valuing*. The middle category, 3.2 *Preference for a value*, is described as the behavior of actively pursuing, wanting, or seeking. This would appear to be the appropriate classification.

If these examples are enough to give the reader an idea of what is involved in classification, perhaps he will wish to try his own hand in the next section and independently attempt to classify some objectives.

Test Yourself on the Classification of These Objectives

The following objectives have been selected from the sample objectives included in Part II. These groups of sample objectives serve as a second type of definition of the subcategory, as well as concretely illustrating the kind of behavior which is implied by the abstract definition. On page 75 will be found the key to the classification of each of these objectives and a page number which indicates where the objective appears in the text. The reader may profit by looking up the page references of these objectives, particularly where one was misclassified or where there was some question about the classification. It may be quite helpful to see the particular objective alongside other objectives classified in the same category. The extended definition of the category given in Part II may also be of value.

The reader will probably wish to refer to the abbreviated version of the *Taxonomy* which appears in Appendix A as he tries to fit these objectives into categories.

1. A sense of responsibility for listening to and participating in public discussion.
2. Begins to form judgments as to the major directions in which American society should move.
3. Observes the traffic rules on foot, on a bicycle, or on another conveyance at intersections and elsewhere.
4. Views problems in objective, realistic, and tolerant terms.
5. Assumes an active role in current literary activities.
6. Finding out and crystallizing the basic assumptions which underlie codes of ethics and are the basis of faith.

7. Develops a conscience.
8. Develops a tolerance for a variety of types of music.
9. Loyalty to the various groups in which one holds membership.
10. Willingness to be of service to the group of which he is a member.
11. Listens for rhythm in poetry or prose read aloud.
12. Enjoys constantly increasing variety of good dramatic and other programs on radio, television, and recordings.

The Classification of Test Items

The essential task in assigning a test item to a category of the *Affective Taxonomy* is to determine what maximum degree of internalization can be assumed from the response situation. The classification of the item is primarily in terms of the manner in which it is stated. Although the actual affective level of the respondent may indeed be higher than the level of the item, we may not infer this when a student chooses the response alternative that is keyed to the particular taxonomic category of the item.

As with cognitive test items, the process of classification of affective items would be facilitated if the classifier had information on both the educational objective and the learning situations which served as the basis for test-item construction.

Let us look at a number of items from the Eight-Year Study's Test 3.32 *Questionnaire on Voluntary Reading.* This is a 100-item questionnaire in which the respondent is asked to read each question and then choose one of three response alternatives: Yes, No, or Uncertain. Generally speaking, the range of the questions in this instrument is represented in the first three categories of the *Affective Taxonomy.*

Do you wish that you had more time to devote to reading?

This is clearly an item at the 1.0 *Receiving* level. It certainly is not at the 2.0 *Responding* level because the item deals with intentions rather than actions. A positive ("Yes") response would indicate that the respondent wishes he had more time to devote to reading. His affirmative answer in no way conveys the notion that he does devote increasing amounts of time to this activity.

If we were to classify this item among the subcategories of the 1.0 *Receiving* category, we would assign it to 1.2 *Willingness to receive.* A "Yes" response to the item suggests something more than 1.1 *Awareness* and something less than 1.3 *Controlled or selected attention,* at least in terms of the manner in which the item is phrased. It suggests a somewhat indefinite positive intention, a willingness or amenability to consider assigning more time to reading. To determine whether the student will or will not devote more time to reading, or in fact has done so already, is the task of other items such as:

Is there a specific block of time after school that you assign to reading?

Do you read at night regularly before going to sleep?

Do you spend a considerable portion of your week ends reading?

Thus this item is classified as 1.2 *Willingness to receive.*

Do you ever spend time browsing in a library or bookstore?

What does it mean when a student reports that from time to time he browses in a library or bookstore? What inferences can we safely make about such behavior? The very act of browsing suggests an affective level higher than 1.0 *Receiving.* Browsing among books generally occurs only after books and reading have been invested with positive affective properties by the browser. Thus this item is certainly at least at the 2.0 *Responding* level. As stated in this form it cannot be classified in the 3.0 *Valuing* category because it does not convey the notion that browsing is an activity that the respondent pursues regularly and with great intensity. He may be a habitual frequenter of libraries and bookstores, but we cannot infer this fact from a "Yes" response to the item as it is stated above.

Within the subcategories of 2.0 *Responding* a "Yes" response should be classified as 2.3 *Satisfaction in response.* The act of browsing certainly suggests a willingness. Rarely is a person forced to browse. Not only is it done willingly; it is accompanied by a positive emotional state which produces satisfaction.

A "No" response to this item clearly indicates a rejection of a minimum amount of browsing. We would therefore consider such a response as being at a taxonomic level lower than 2.3 *Satisfaction in response.*

After you have read a book, are you usually interested in finding out what critics have said about it?

A desire to learn about critical comments on books read suggests an attitude toward reading that is more sophisticated than just obtaining satisfaction from it. Clearly the act of reading is here more than an end in itself; it is a steppingstone to other activities. A "Yes" response to this item is clearly in the 3.0 *Valuing* category. But since the activity described in this item is, relatively speaking, less sophisticated than, let us say, writing a critique of the book, we would classify a "Yes" response as 3.1 *Acceptance of a value*.

Is it rather unusual for you to compare two or more books and come to a decision about the relative merits of each?

Here voluntary reading has become so important to the respondent that it leads to the employment of higher cognitive processes, such as comparison and evaluation. A "No" response to this item, which indicates that it is usual for the respondent to compare and evaluate books read, belongs at an affective taxonomic level slightly higher than the reading-of-the-critics behavior of the previous example. Thus we classify this item as 3.2 *Preference for a value*.

Is there any author whom you like so well that you would wish to read any new book he might publish?

This item should be classified as 3.3 *Commitment*. The decision of a student to read everything written by a particular author is evidence of a deep commitment not only to the author but to reading.

Have any of the books which you have read made you want to do something about such problems as crime, poverty, or unemployment?

When books have succeeded in arousing impulses to take action, we are witnessing not only the power of the printed word to arouse strong emotions but also a person who has become sufficiently involved in his reading that compelling emotional forces are liberated. We can therefore also classify a "Yes" response to this item as representing 3.3 *Commitment*.

The highest level of the *Affective Taxonomy* represented in the *Questionnaire on Voluntary Reading* is 3.3 *Commitment*. To give the reader a sense of items on reading at the 4.0 *Organization* level of the *Affective Taxonomy* let us turn to the *Inventory H-B2, Satisfactions Found in Reading Fiction*, of the Cooperative Study in General Education. Part I of this instrument consists of 150 statements to each of which the respondent can make one of three responses: (1) that the statement applies to his reading of fiction; (2) that the statement does not apply to his reading of fiction; (3) that he is uncertain whether the statement applies to his reading of fiction.

Finding attitudes toward life expressed which I can adopt in my own philosophy of life.

For the student who reports that this statement does apply to his reading of fiction we can infer that he is attempting to conceptualize powerful ideas which he has found in his reading. Since he has not begun to incorporate them into his general value system, this is classified as 4.1 *Conceptualization of a value.*

Being encouraged by finding that other people are apparently troubled by the same sorts of problems and difficulties I am.

Here again reading is used to derive ideas about the human condition and the conduct of life. No inference can be made directly from the statement as to whether such a discovery made in reading fiction has gone beyond the "thinking about" stage and has been incorporated into the value system. Thus the classification category of the statement is 4.1 *Conceptualization of a value.*

In this first edition of the *Affective Taxonomy* we shall not ask the reader to attempt to classify items representative of the very highest levels of the *Taxonomy.* There are two reasons for this: first, the 5.0 *Characterization* category represents the deeper and more general levels of personality structure. These are levels to which the formal instructional effort does not address itself directly. Second, measurement that represents behavior at this level consists of a scale containing a number of items rather than an individual item. Examples of such scales are given in Part II.

Test Yourself on the Classification of Items

Each of the following ten test items to be classified is presented in Part II as illustrative of the characteristic behaviors of a particular level of the *Affective Taxonomy.* Classify them in terms of a student choosing the response alternative with an asterisk. The key to the classification of these items is on page 75.

1. Is it rather unusual for you to read books, magazines, or newspapers for the particular purpose of learning more about authors and their works?

   (a) Yes
   *(b) No
   (c) Uncertain

2. Do you attend public meetings to protest against something which you regard as unfair?

   *(a) Occasionally or frequently
   (b) Never

3. Is it usually difficult for you to read for as long as an hour without becoming bored?

   (a) Yes
   *(b) No
   (c) Uncertain

4. What is your opinion of this unsettled question?

   In deciding whether a law is constitutional, the Supreme Court should consider the contributions of the law to the welfare of the people as more important than its strict agreement with the Constitution.

   *(a) I agree with the statement.
   (b) I disagree with the statement.
   (c) I don't know how I feel about the statement.

5. What is your opinion of this statement?

   One should adjust his diet until his weight conforms (within 3 to 4 pounds) to the figure given in height-age-weight tables.

   *(a) I agree with the statement.
   (b) I disagree with the statement.
   (c) I don't know how I feel about the statement.

6. Do you read books chiefly because your parents or teachers urge you to do so?

   *(a) Yes
   (b) No
   (c) Uncertain

7. Would you like to know more about the history and development of some type of literature, such as the drama or short story?

   *(a) Yes
   (b) No
   (c) Uncertain

8. Once you have begun a book, do you usually finish reading it within a few days' time?

   *(a) Yes
   (b) No

9. Verdi wrote *Aida, Rigoletto, La Traviata,* and *Carmen.*

   (a) True
   *(b) False

10. In your opinion, can a man who works in business all the week best spend Sunday in (rank the responses in order of attractiveness):

*(a) trying to educate himself by reading serious books.
*(b) trying to win at golf, or racing.
*(c) going to an orchestral concert.
*(d) hearing a really good sermon.

Key to the Classification of Affective-Domain Objectives

1. 3.1 (p. 141)
2. 4.2 (p. 159)
3. 2.1 (p. 120)
4. 5.1 (p. 167)
5. 3.2 (p. 145)
6. 4.1 (p. 156)
7. 5.2 (p. 171)
8. 1.2 (p. 108)
9. 3.3 (p. 149)
10. 2.2 (p. 126)
11. 1.3 (p. 113)
12. 2.3 (p. 132)

Experience with a similar exercise in the cognitive area has led us to conclude that classification in the appropriate sub-category is a much less objective process than classification in the major category. Perhaps we should be satisfied if we can get this much agreement.

Key to the Classification of Affective-Domain Test Items

(The page numbers indicate where in Part II the item appears in context with others of the same *Taxonomy* level.)

1. 2.2 (p. 129)
2. 3.3 (p. 152)
3. 1.2 (p. 111)
4. 4.1 (p. 158)
5. 3.1 (p. 144)
6. 2.1 (p. 124)
7. 1.3 (p. 115)
8. 2.3 (p. 137)
9. 1.1 (p. 106)
10. 4.2 (p. 163)

CHAPTER 6

A NEW LOOK AT CURRICULUM, EVALUATION, AND RESEARCH

As we review the uses to which the first volume of the *Taxonomy* (*Cognitive Domain*) has been put, it seems to us that its main contribution has been the increased development of operational definitions of educational objectives. The *Taxonomy* has been used by teachers, curriculum builders, and educational research workers as one device to attack the problem of specifying in detail the expected outcomes of the learning process. When educational objectives are stated in operational and detailed form, it is possible to make appropriate evaluation instruments and to determine, with some precision, which learning experiences are likely to be of value in promoting the development of the objective and which are likely to be of little or no value.[1]

It is this increased specificity which we hope will be promoted by the *Affective Domain* part of the *Taxonomy*. Educational objectives in this domain tend to be statements of desirable but undefined virtues. As long as the affective objectives remain in this empty and airy limbo, there is little that is likely to be done in the school either in evaluation or in the providing of appropriate learning experiences. If affective objectives can be defined with appropriate precision, we believe it may be no more difficult to produce changes in students in this domain than it has been in the cognitive domain. We do recognize that the problems are different and that much will have to be done by

[1]The advent of programmed instruction has made us more aware of the fact that objectives may be developed at different levels of abstraction. Objectives which are specific enough for curriculum building are not specific enough for programming. But the detailed specifications of behavior needed for programming are so specific and therefore so numerous as to prevent one's "seeing the forest for the trees." Though probably excellent for daily instructional plans, they are too minute for curriculum building. We need objectives at various levels as we translate the very broad and general objectives of education into the specific ones which provide guidance for the development of step-by-step learning experiences. The *Taxonomy* deals with objectives at the curriculum-construction level.

teachers, curriculum specialists, and research workers before this domain becomes as well understood as the cognitive domain is at present.

In the cognitive domain there is ample evidence that the lowest level of the domain—the knowledge objectives—can be achieved by a great variety of learning experiences. Basically, all that seems to be required for the development of knowledge objectives is an attentive and well-motivated learner and a set of learning experiences in which an accurate version of a piece of information is communicated to the student by means of the printed page, the spoken word, or the use of pictures and illustrations. Given this view of the nature of learning experiences required for the knowledge objectives, it is relatively easy to understand why so many of the research studies—on large and small classes, teaching by television vs. teaching by regular classroom procedures, lectures vs. discussions, demonstrations vs. laboratory experiences, the use of programmed learning materials or audiovisual techniques, and even the independent use of books and other printed materials—all give very similar results when measured by appropriate tests and other techniques for evaluating the student's achievement of information.

The more complex and higher categories of the cognitive domain require far more sophisticated learning experiences than the simple communication of a correct version of an idea or event to the student. Much more motivation is required, much more activity and participation on the part of the learner is necessary, and more opportunities must be available to help the individual to gain insight into the processes he uses as well as misuses if these more complex objectives are to be achieved. Chausow (1955), Dressel and Mayhew (1954), Bloom (1954), and others have made clear that the achievement of complex types of critical thinking objectives are not likely to be attained by a simple lecture method or by merely telling the students what they are to do or how they are to do it. Demonstrations of appropriate problem-solving processes are not very effective in bringing about actual problem-solving competence. Dressel and Mayhew (1954) show that only small gains are attained in critical thinking when merely a single course in a college program aims to develop this type of competence. On the other hand, when the entire curriculum is devoted to this same purpose (i.e., when these objectives become the theme that plays through a large number of courses) the students' gains in critical thinking become very large. In effect, the entire educational environment must be turned toward the achievement of complex objectives if they are to be attained in any significant way.

We believe the same principles probably apply to the affective domain. The lowest level, which is the receiving of and attending to new material, probably requires little more than the effective presentation of the material to which the student is to attend. What seems to be needed is an interested student, who is prepared to receive the necessary communications and ideas, and an effective presentation of the material under conditions of minimum distraction and interference from other cues and stimuli. Through this process students can become aware of new musical and artistic forms, new relations among people, etc. Through a variety of learning experiences the student can become aware of and willing to receive new material, or at least give it attention.

The securing of the appropriate responses from the individual, such as those defined under our second category, requires that the new cues and stimuli be received under conditions that make it easy for the individual to respond and give him satisfaction from the act of responding. This also should not be very difficult, provided that the teacher himself is able to get satisfaction from the responses and to communicate not only the process of responding but also something of the rewards to be received from the appropriate responses to the stimuli and cues.

However, as we turn to the objectives which go beyond merely receiving or responding to stimuli and cues, we find that the development of learning experiences that are appropriate requires far more effort and far more complex sets of arrangements than are usually provided in particular classroom lessons and sessions. We do not think that we have all the research needed to understand thoroughly the process by which the more complex and difficult affective objectives can be attained, but we do believe that there are many suggestions provided by research in this and related areas. In the following section we shall review a few of the important studies that bear on this problem. We do recognize that a great deal of new research is needed if we are to understand how the more complex and, we believe, more significant educational objectives in the affective domain are to be achieved.

Before considering some of the research, we should point out the high cost in energy, time, and commitment of achieving complex objectives in either the cognitive or the affective domain. Such objectives are not to be attained simply by someone expressing the desire that they be attained or by a few sessions of class time devoted to the attainment of the objectives. It is clear that the educators who wish to achieve these more complex objectives must be willing to pay the rather great price entailed. This is merely an admonition against the claim that a particular school or college achieves certain complex objectives, when the staff is not fully committed to doing the necessary work for the development of appropriate learning experiences and evaluation evidence. This means that as objectives are claimed which are classifiable in the higher categories of either the cognitive or the affective domain, there must be a great involvement on the part of the staff as well as administrators in attaining the objectives. Such objectives should not be stated lightly and expected to be achieved by some semimagical process in the ordinary course of events. Stating an objective and achieving it are two very different things.

If this admonition is heeded, one might expect a smaller number of objectives to be claimed which are classified in the higher categories of the cognitive or affective domain. It also means that all the educational objectives stated by a particular faculty or staff are not of the same order. That is, there must be some hierarchical ordering of objectives such that the most important objectives are given high priority and emphasis while less important and less central objectives may be given lower priority and less time and effort by all concerned. All too frequently a list of objectives is stated in which many different kinds of objectives are desired or expected to be achieved, but there is little in the way of ordering of these objectives. It is likely that the higher the objective in the classification scheme, the more time and effort will be required for its attainment. It is to be expected that some objectives may take several years to be reached to a significant degree. Other objectives are likely to be gained only if they are emphasized and reinforced in different parts of the curriculum simultaneously. The ordering of objectives is of importance in both domains, but we regard it as of prime importance in the affective domain.

The emphasis on a hierarchical ordering of objectives should not be taken to mean that we believe the more complex objectives in the affective domain can be attained without achieving some of the relevant less complex or less internalized objectives. The entire domain proceeds from categories which are relatively simple, requiring very little from the student, to categories of objectives which require a fairly complete internalization of a set of attitudes, values, and behaviors. We imagine that the learning of the more highly internalized objectives must start with the more simple and perhaps superficial behaviors specified in the first few categories of this domain. It is entirely possible that the learning of the more difficult and internalized objectives must be in the form of a "loop" which begins with the simpler and more overt behaviors, gradually moves to the more complex and more internalized behaviors, and repeats the entire procedure in new areas of content and behavior until a highly internalized, consistent, and complex set of affective behaviors is finally developed.

Every teacher attempts to evaluate the changes that he has made in his students, and it is clearly entirely possible for him to do so successfully at the lower levels of the *Taxonomy*. But a teacher will rarely have the same students over a sufficient period of time to make measurable changes in certain affective behaviors. Some objectives, particularly the complex ones at the top of the affective continuum, are probably attained as the product of all, or at least a major portion, of a student's years in school. Thus measures of a semester's or year's growth would reveal little change. This suggests that an evaluation plan covering at least several grades and involving the coordinated efforts of several teachers is probably a necessity. A plan involving all the grades in a system is likely to be even more effective. Such efforts would permit gathering longitudinal data on the same students so that gains in complex objectives would be measurable. Patterns of growth in relation to various school efforts would be revealed. Planned evaluation efforts to measure certain cognitive objectives on a longitudinal basis are to be found in some school systems, particularly where they use achievement test batteries designed to facilitate this. Similar efforts with respect to affective objectives are quite rare. If we are serious about attaining complex affective objectives, we shall have to build coordinated evaluation programs that trace the successes and failures of our efforts to achieve them.

Achievement of Affective Objectives and Behaviors

We regret the lack of research dealing directly with clear-cut affective objectives of the schools. While there are some studies which bear rather directly on affective behaviors, there are relatively few studies which fit neatly into our taxonomic scheme. However, we have selected a few studies which appear to us to make it clear that affective objectives *can be achieved by the schools* if the attainment of such objectives is regarded as sufficiently important by teachers and administrators.

One of the important pieces of research in relation not only to developing an awareness of a particular idea but also to producing actual changes in overt behavior is to be found in a report by Kurt Lewin (1947). In a study for the National Research Council during the war years, Lewin was interested in finding a way of changing the food habits of a group of women. He wished to get them to use certain meats as well as other foods which the women were not in the habit of using. Lewin found that a lecture on the merits of the new foods produced little or no change in the actual food habits of the women. On the other hand, a group discussion about the foods and the problems of using them as well as a verbal commitment from the women to use the new foods resulted in a change of food habits by a considerable proportion of the women. Follow-up studies made four or more weeks later showed that the women were still using the new foods.

The point of this study is that exhortations, a rational argument for a particular behavior, and passive participation of a group of persons is likely to lead to little more than an awareness of the new material and perhaps even some intellectual conviction about the appropriateness of the new behavior. However, for any major reorganization of actual practices and responses to take place, the individual must be able to examine his own feelings and attitudes on the subject, bring them out into the open, see how they compare with the feelings and views of others, and move from an intellectual awareness of a particular behavior or practice to an actual commitment to the new practice. It is of interest to note that the amount of time required for the discussion and interaction type of communication was no greater than that required for a straightforward presentation of the merits of the new practices.

What is suggested here, if specific changes are to take place in the learners, is that the learning experiences must be of a two-way nature in which both students and teacher are involved in an interactive manner, rather than having one present something to be "learned" by the other.

Newcomb (1943), in his study at Bennington College, was interested in the impact of the college on the social liberalism of the students. He found that at this college for women the faculty was very much committed to developing more socially liberal attitudes on the part of the students. Social liberalism was the major theme that ran through the curriculum and the extracurricular activities. It was emphasized not only in the social-sciences course but in other interactions between teachers and students, in the dormitory relations, and in many other activities on the campus. Newcomb found that, on the average, the girls at Bennington became more liberal as they progressed through the four years. There were some who were able to resist the effects of this basic theme running through the entire college environment and who changed very little while they were at the college. For the most part the students who did not change significantly were individuals who were not in effective communication with the larger environment. That is, they tended to be individuals whose own emotional problems were so great that they did not interact effectively with the larger environment, or they consisted of small groups of girls who found a smaller environment in which they could operate. These girls formed limited clique groups which were somewhat isolated from the more central activities in the college as a whole. Newcomb's research suggests that a very powerful environment can make for significant growth or change in a complex affective objective and that this growth or change in attitudes will be sustained for some time after the college experience.[2]

Teachers and other adults in the home or school sometimes blithely assume that they are the significant figures in the environment. This is probably true in the child's early years, but it becomes less true as the individual frees himself from the domination or control of adults. The work of Coleman (1961) in suburban schools in the Midwest demonstrates very clearly that during the adolescent period, under some conditions, the peer group has a greater effect on the students than do teachers and,

[2]Newcomb is currently undertaking a twenty-year follow-up study of the Bennington students.

perhaps, parents. Thus Coleman found that the students at the adolescent stage were very frequently responding to what they believed was expected or valued by the peer group rather than by the adults. Their motivation for educational achievement, and their social practices and habits were more nearly controlled by their peers than by their elders.

A similar finding is emerging from the study of enrichment of educational opportunities in the New York public schools, which has been termed "Higher Horizons" (Mayer, 1961). In this study a group of about 350 students beginning with the seventh or eighth grade have been given special opportunities to visit art galleries, museums, operas, etc. and to go on field trips to colleges and other places. These students have been assigned to special classes consisting of a dozen or so pupils. They have been given a great deal of individual attention by the teachers. In addition, they have been provided with far more counseling and guidance than they would usually receive in the schools. It is significant that a sizable proportion of these students are responding to the new practices and are developing positive attitudes and values toward education and educational opportunity, while this has not occurred in the control groups who were not given such special opportunities.

The significant thing to remember in this very ambitious project is that the major impact of the new program is to develop attitudes and values toward learning which are not shared by the parents and guardians or by the peer group in the neighborhood. There are many stories of the conflict and tension that these new practices are producing between parents and children. There is even more conflict between the students and the members of their peer groups who are not participating in the special opportunities. The effectiveness of this new set of environmental conditions is probably related to the extent to which the students are "isolated" from both the home and the peer group during this period of time. It is unlikely that such "separation" from the home and peer group would take place after the age of sixteen or seventeen. And it is also likely that the earlier the new environments are created the more effective they will be.

Our concern here is not with the desirability of the new attitudes and values and whether it is appropriate to attempt to replace earlier sets of attitudes by newer ones. From the operational point of view and from the research point of view, it does seem clear that, to create effectively a new set of attitudes and values, the individual must undergo great reorganization of his personal beliefs and attitudes and he must be involved in an environment which in many ways is separated from the previous environment in which he has developed. Similar findings are evident in the Puerto Rican Studies (Morrison, 1958) in New York City.

While we have emphasized the deliberate creating of a new environment to bring about specific changes in either the cognitive or affective domain, there is evidence that some changes may be wrought without this conscious and deliberate effort to create a special environment. Plant (1958) in his study of the authoritarianism at San José College and Dressel and Mayhew (1954) in their study of this same pattern in a number of colleges indicate that there are significant decreases in the authoritarianism among students who are in a general college environment which does not deliberately seek to bring about these changes. It is likely that many of these changes are produced by association with peers who have less authoritarian points of view, as well as through the impact of a great many courses of study in which the authoritarian pattern is in some ways brought into question while more rational and nonauthoritarian behaviors are emphasized. However, we should be quick to point out that the changes produced in such a general academic atmosphere which is not deliberately created are probably of smaller magnitude than the changes produced where the entire environment is organized (deliberately or not) with a particular theme at work. In summary, we find that learning experiences which are highly organized and interrelated may produce major changes in behavior related to complex objectives in both the cognitive and affective domain. Such new objectives can best be attained where the individual is separated from earlier environmental conditions and when he is in association with a group of peers who are changing in much the same direction and who thus tend to reinforce each other.

In his studies of stability and change in various characteristics, Bloom (1964) finds that the individual is more open to some of these major changes earlier in the growth period than later. The research on social class and learning, as well as the evidence on social class and basic sets of attitudes and values, suggests that the early environment—that is, the early environment in the home as well as the school—may more effectively produce significant changes in basic attitudes than are likely to be produced later in the career of the individual.

The evidence points quite convincingly to the fact that age is a factor operating against attempts to effect a complete or thoroughgoing reorganization of attitudes and values. We would be far more pessimistic about attempts to bring about major changes in the higher categories of the affective domain in adults than we would about making them in young children. It is quite possible that the adolescent period, with its biological and other modifications, is a stage in which more change can be produced than in many other periods of the individual's career. Super and Overstreet (1960) do find that there is an increasing stability of interests in the age period of about ten to fifteen and that appropriate learning experiences and counseling and guidance may do much to develop different kinds of interests. Dressel (1954) points to the increased stability of interests in the late adolescent and early college period, but he takes the view that the stability of these interests is the result of the continuity and similarity of learning experiences over this time period. Also, he believes that a major change in learning and other experiences will produce less stability of interests.

Relationships between the Cognitive and Affective Domains

We recognize that human behavior can rarely be neatly compartmentalized in terms of cognition and affect. It is easier to divide educational objectives and intended behaviors into these two domains. However, even the separation of objectives into these two groups is somewhat artificial in that no teacher or curriculum worker really intends one entirely without the other.

There is a great deal of research which demonstrates that cognition and affect can never be completely separated (Barker *et al.*, 1941; Bloom and Broder, 1950; Johnson, 1955; Russell, 1956; Thistlethwaite, 1950; Wertheimer, 1945). But even more interesting are the possibilities that one is in large part the effect of the other.

There have been many who take the view that interest will arise from increased *information* about some area of knowledge—

that if we will forget all about the affective objectives, they will "naturally" arise from the development of the cognitive objectives. More recently a number of workers (e.g., Bruner, 1960) have felt that it is the process of problem solving and discovery in learning that will bring about increased motivation for the subject and all the appropriate interests and attitudes. Their view is that it is not so much what is learned, but how it is learned, which will determine the affective objectives that will be attained at the same time as the cognitive objectives.

There are also some educators who believe that the primary problem is one of motivating students. If the students develop appropriate affective behaviors, then the learning of the subject matter (and cognitive objectives) will take place at a very rapid rate and at a high level of complexity.

The writers are persuaded that, although there may be varying relations between cognitive and affective objectives, the particular relations in any situation are determined by the learning experiences the students have had. Thus one set of learning experiences may produce a high level of cognitive achievement at the same time that it produces an actual distaste for the subject. Another set of learning experiences may produce a high level of cognitive achievement as well as great interest and liking for the subject. Still a third set of learning experiences may produce relatively low levels of cognitive achievement but a high degree of interest and liking for the subject.

We suspect that all three situations are not only theoretically but actually possible. What is true in any given situation has rarely been investigated because we have not had the necessary instruments to study both cognitive and affective outcomes simultaneously. It is to be hoped that an increased emphasis on affective objectives and the development of appropriate instruments and research designs will enable educational research workers to resolve some of these issues in both theoretical and more practical and specific educational situations.

Some Additional Research Problems

Perhaps the central research problem posed by the affective domain is how to evaluate affective objectives with greater validity, reliability, and objectivity. In this volume we cite many techniques for appraising such objectives, but we are fully aware of the fact that much must be done before the development of testing techniques in the affective domain will reach the rather high state of clarity and precision which is now possible in the cognitive domain. This is not to say that all is well in the testing of cognitive objectives. A great deal of research in testing methods is still necessary for this domain. However, the state of the art of testing is far more fully developed in the cognitive domain than is at present true in the affective domain. If we could justify the publication of this volume on no other ground than as an incentive to do more research on the appraisal of affective objectives, we believe the endeavor represented by this publication would be fully warranted.

The work of Sanford and others (1956) on the Vassar campus and that of Webster (1958) at the Center for the Study of Higher Education in California suggest some of the directions for this research. Throughout this volume we have suggested some of the problems of constructing evaluation instruments for the affective domain. We are of the opinion that, as better evaluation instruments are developed, we shall be able to see much more clearly what types of environments and learning experiences produce change and which do not, or at least to understand better the conditions and limitations for change in the affective domain. More important, perhaps, is the utility of the evaluation techniques in making more explicit what is meant by a particular objective, so that one may come to perceive much more concretely what the goal or objective really is as well as some of the requirements for its attainment.

Another research problem to which we have already referred in the preceding section is what learning experiences produce what changes in the affective (as well as in the cognitive) domain. This, it seems to us, is a key problem in education, and until it is attacked on a theoretical as well as a practical basis we shall either avoid concern for affective objectives or pursue them with great but ill-informed intensity. Speculations rather than theory, and argument rather than evidence, appear to guide what feeble efforts are now made to develop affective objectives in students.

Are affective objectives influenced by specific learning experiences, or are they influenced primarily by the total environment (in as well as out of school)? Coleman (1961) points to the effectiveness of the out-of-school environment on attitudes toward school learning. Many other works could be cited on the same point. Pace and Stern (1958) point to some of the techniques by which educational environments may be studied and measured. Much must be done before we can determine the consequences of particular learning experiences as well as the consequences of the large school and out-of-school environment.

Maslow (1959) has suggested that peak experience may have a powerful influence on major changes in the individual. The hypothesis arising out of Maslow's work is that a single powerful experience may have much more impact on the individual than many less powerful experiences. One of the writers (Bloom) has been attempting to do research on what might be called *peak learning experiences*. Although this problem has been explored in only a cursory way, the evidence collected so far suggests that a single hour of classroom activity under certain conditions may bring about a major reorganization in cognitive as well as affective behaviors. We are of the opinion that this will prove to be a most fruitful area of research in connection with the affective domain. It may very well help us to understand some of the conditions that are necessary for major changes in learners in affective objectives. It may also help us to recognize that not all hours of student-teacher-material interaction are of equal value.

An obvious research problem for the affective domain has to do with development over time and the retention of change. The research reported in *Handbook I: Cognitive Domain* reveals that the developments in some cognitive objectives are retained for only relatively short periods of time while the competence in other objectives is retained over a very long while. Newcomb (1943) suggests that social liberalism is likely to be retained after college only when the environment reinforces these attitudes. Strong (1955) finds that some occupational interests persist for twenty or more years. Nelson (1954), Kelly (1955), and Bender (1958) show that some values are retained over long periods while others are subject to marked change after the college years. It seems clear that the retention of affective changes produced in the schools is a function of how early in the individual's career the objective was developed, how deep-seated the learning has been, and the environmental forces to which the individual is subjected over the school and postschool years (Darley, 1938).

As we have classified educational objectives in the affective domain, it is assumed that the higher objectives are more ingrained and internalized. They are, as described, more pervasive. This would suggest that there should be more transfer of training for the higher categories and more compartmentalization for the lower categories. These assumptions must be empirically tested. Research on these different levels of the affective domain should reveal the extent to which these assumptions hold under different conditions. Is it possible for an individual to develop some of the more highly internalized behaviors without changing the entire personality of the person? Can individuals be psychologically healthy and still hold basic values which are not consistent, psychologically as well as logically?

But perhaps an even more fundamental need in this area is for research directed toward understanding the underlying process by which individuals undergo change in the affective domain. The writings of Asch (1952) on the shaping of attitudes reveal something of the process of interaction between the individual and the environment which brings about the major changes. Charlotte Towle (1954), in her study of the basic reorganization of the attitudes and values of social workers, reveals something of the psychoanalytic and psychological processes at work in the reshaping and reorganization of basic attitudes. What seems to be evident in some of this work is that the individual must in part isolate himself from his earlier environment and even in part deny his own basic self and his own basic attitudes.

Allport (1954) emphasizes the basic reorganization that must take place in the individual if really new values and character traits are to be formed. We are of the opinion that as we come to understand this process we may find ways of helping bring about major changes in the affective domain with less in the way of trauma and conflict than now seems to be the case. Is it possible for individuals to take on the new without rejecting the old? Is it possible that programs of the Higher Horizons type (Mayer, 1961) help individuals become motivated toward higher education and the new values involved in academic work without at the same time bringing about great conflict and tension between the individual and his home? We believe that it is this area of the affective domain that touches all of us as we attempt to alter our basic attitudes and values toward members of other social and racial groups. Each of us needs to look around to find what is happening to others and perhaps to look at himself to see the basic reorganization of attitudes that is going on within him and the complexities and difficulties it creates.

However, back of all the more operational and psychological problems is the basic question of what changes are desirable and appropriate. Here is where the philosopher, as well as the behavioral scientist, must find ways of determining what changes are desirable and perhaps what changes are necessary. If we are to muster the tremendous effort and resources required to bring about basic changes in the more complex affective behaviors, we must be certain of the importance and desirability of these new objectives. It is not enough merely to desire a new objective or to wish others to be molded in the image that we find desirable or satisfactory. We must find ways of understanding and determining what objectives are central and significant if we are to summon the appropriate effort to achieve these more complex objectives. One might hope that indications of the cost of achieving them would stop many educators from seriously hoping for and desiring any set of objectives that come to mind in a half-hour session devoted to thinking about new objectives for the school. New objectives are important, but they must be thought through very carefully, and all must be willing to pay the price if they are to be obtained.

While the psychologist and the philosopher may have views on what is desirable and even necessary in the affective domain, there is still the question of what affective objectives society will permit and even encourage. Our own society has fluctuated as to the affective objectives it will permit the school to develop. Political and social forces are constantly at work, pressing the schools for some affective objectives and just as constantly placing restrictions on the school with regard to others. The play of these forces has, in many instances, made teachers and school administrators wary of expressing these objectives and all too frequently has led school staffs to retreat to the somewhat less dangerous cognitive domain. Can the schools take the initiative in the affective domain, or must they approach it with great caution and hesitation? We leave this problem to the curriculum makers, the educational philosophers, and the social and political forces which may or may not make certain objectives clearly desirable and even necessary.

The affective domain is, in retrospect, a virtual "Pandora's Box." One finds in it the objectives which were stated confidently at one time and then allowed to disappear from view. One finds in it the objectives on which disagreement is most likely within a school. One finds in it the vital points on which the society itself may be in disagreement. Much of the affective domain has been repressed, denied, and obscured. It is as though we have come upon the unconscious and begun to examine its contents. We are not entirely sure that opening our "box" is necessarily a good thing; we are certain that it is not likely to be a source of peace and harmony among the members of a school staff.

Some would question the desirability of a school's considering affective objectives. Some would wonder about the wisdom of making these objectives explicit rather than implicit, and more would doubt the possibility of the school's doing anything significant to develop affective objectives. If we obscure the objectives in the affective domain and bury them in platitudes, how can we examine them, determine their meaning, or do anything constructive about them? Our "box" must be opened if we are to face reality and take action.

It is in this "box" that the most influential controls are to be found. The affective domain contains the forces that determine the nature of an individual's life and ultimately the life of an entire people. To keep the "box" closed is to deny the existence of the powerful motivational forces that shape the life of each of us. To look the other way is to avoid coming to terms with the real. Education is not the rote memorization of meaningless material to be regurgitated on an examination paper. Perhaps the two *Taxonomy* structures may help us to see the awesome possibilities of the relations between students-ideas-teachers.

PART II
THE AFFECTIVE DOMAIN TAXONOMY

THE CLASSIFICATION SCHEME
ILLUSTRATIVE EDUCATIONAL OBJECTIVES
ILLUSTRATIVE TEST ITEMS

Introduction

This section describes the categories of the classification scheme and gives examples of educational objectives and test items which illustrate each category. The categories are intended to be hierarchical in order, arranged along a continuum of internalization from lowest to highest.

The categories and their subdivisions are:

- 1.0 Receiving (attending)
  - 1.1 Awareness
  - 1.2 Willingness to receive
  - 1.3 Controlled or selected attention
- 2.0 Responding
  - 2.1 Acquiescence in responding
  - 2.2 Willingness to respond
  - 2.3 Satisfaction in response
- 3.0 Valuing
  - 3.1 Acceptance of a value
  - 3.2 Preference for a value
  - 3.3 Commitment (conviction)
- 4.0 Organization
  - 4.1 Conceptualization of a value
  - 4.2 Organization of a value system
- 5.0 Characterization by a value or value complex
  - 5.1 Generalized set
  - 5.2 Characterization

Each section contains a brief description of the category and its position in the *Taxonomy* hierarchy. These category descriptions are supplemented by illustrative educational objectives and test items. In addition, there is a section on the evaluation of the achievement of objectives in the category, the chief purpose of which is to consider some of the major issues in constructing instruments to measure the behaviors of the category.

The categorization of illustrative objectives presents many of the same problems in this domain as in the cognitive. The experiences which precede the learning of a given objective, as much as the nature of the behavior described, will often be a prime determining factor in where it is best categorized. The location of the present samples of objectives is based on the combined judgment of a small group of people who could agree on their best placement. It is possible that future users will perceive appropriate changes in the location of some of them or perhaps drop some as being not precise enough for categorization. The reader is encouraged to contact the authors if he has suggestions for modifications in the categories or alternative classifications of particular illustrations. The reasons for these modifications should be most helpful in planning revisions of the category statements and in clarifying the illustrations.[1]

Wherever possible, illustrative test items are taken from existing instruments. Quite often these illustrations have been modified to reflect, in a more precise manner, a category of the affective domain.

A serious limitation in providing illustrative test items for this Handbook is the relative scarcity of published instruments which have been expressly designed to measure affective outcomes of instruction. Although there are affective consequences of all teaching-learning activities, and although representative statements of objectives of local curricula often contain hopes for affective as well as cognitive outcomes, the typical school examines for cognitive changes only.

There is another limitation with regard to illustrative test materials in the affective domain. This is the overwhelming preponderance of instruments in the humanities—literature (including reading), music, and art. There is almost a complete absence of instruments to measure affective outcomes of instruction in the various physical and biological sciences, in mathematics, and in the social studies. This is true at the college level as well as at the secondary and elementary levels. We have tried to correct this imbalance somewhat by devising illustrations for these latter curriculum areas. Such illustrations appear in the sections devoted to issues and strategies for testing at the various taxonomic levels.

Few illustrative test items were drawn from the large number of tests of interests and personality which are used in the guidance and counseling programs of many secondary schools and colleges. It is true that these are tests which belong in the affective domain, but they do not directly measure specific affective outcomes of

---

[1]The objectives used as illustrations in Part II were taken, in the main, from a large number of course syllabi and from statements of the educational objectives of school districts. These objectives are presented for illustrative purposes only. We do not wish the reader to assume that an educational objective which is cited is therefore a significant one.

school learning so much as the general level of development of the socialization process.

Fortunately for the writing of this Handbook, a number of major studies of curriculum effectiveness produced, as part of their evaluation phases, a large variety of tests designed specifically to measure affective outcomes of instruction in particular subjects. The authors leaned heavily on the instruments, mostly unpublished, of two of these studies—the Eight-Year Study of the Progressive Education Association (1933-41) and the Cooperative Study in General Education of the American Council on Education (1939-44).

1.0 RECEIVING (ATTENDING)

At this level we are concerned that the learner be sensitized to the existence of certain phenomena and stimuli; that is, that he be willing to receive or to attend to them. To the uninitiated, Bach is repetitive and boring. To those who have been sensitized to listening to this type of music, it is intricate and complex. However, even the unsophisticated can recognize that in some of his works there are "rounds," if they are aware of what to listen for. The teacher who makes the student conscious of such a characteristic in Bach's work is accomplishing the lowest level of behavior in this category.

Often the teacher will create artificial situations so that the student can more easily distinguish what he is to attend to. The music teacher may play the main theme on the piano, then repeat it as a round so the student can recognize it when it is played by the full orchestra. Many audiovisual devices similarly simplify the situation so that the point of emphasis is readily apparent to the student.

Since the achievement at each step in a hierarchy determines achievement at the next higher one, clearly this, the first or bottom step, is indispensable if the student is to be properly oriented toward the teacher's sequence of instruction. For instance, unless the student is aware of different moods in music, of variation in accent, beat, and rhythm, of different hues and saturation of colors, the teacher cannot proceed to help the child value these phenomena or, in the teacher's terminology, "appreciate" them.

To indicate that this is the bottom rung of the ladder is not to imply that the teacher is starting *de novo*. Because of previous experience (formal or informal), the student brings to each situation a point of view or set which may facilitate or hinder his recognition of that to which the teacher is trying to sensitize him. Some of this previous learning is in the cognitive area.

Less obvious, however, is the effect of learning in the values and emotions area. The effects of values and emotions on perception have been intensively studied, and the research indicates clearly the influence of previous learning on perception. For instance, tachistoscopic presentations of words which are socially unacceptable indicate that longer viewing periods are necessary for them to be perceived than for words which are, for the subject, neutral or positively loaded. When unacceptable material is momentarily flashed on the screen along with words that are neutral or positively oriented, the latter are more frequently and accurately perceived. Often, unacceptable material is distorted by the subject, who makes it more acceptable in his reporting through the addition, deletion, or substitution of letters.

That such a phenomenon operates in the classroom is no news to the teacher. It will certainly influence his means of teaching for objectives at the *Receiving* level. The effects noted above are not the effects sought in the objectives. They are part of the behavior that occurs in the learning guided toward specific objectives, and they are noted here as a part of the learning process, not as a part of the behavior in the category.

The category *Receiving* has been divided into three subcategories to indicate three different levels of attending to phenomena. The subcategories are arbitrary divisions on a continuum. From an extremely passive position or role on the part of the learner, where the sole responsibility for the evocation of the behavior rests with the teacher—that is, the responsibility rests with him for "capturing" the student's attention—the continuum extends to a point at which the learner directs his attention, at least at a semiconscious level, toward the preferred stimuli.

1.1 Awareness

Though it is the bottom rung of the affective domain, *Awareness* is almost a cognitive behavior. But unlike *Knowledge*, the lowest level of the cognitive domain, we are not so much concerned with a memory of, or ability to recall, an item or fact as we are that, given appropriate opportunity, the learner will merely be conscious of something—that he take into account a situation, phenomenon, object, or state of affairs. Like *Knowledge* it does not imply an assessment of the qualities or nature of the stimulus, but unlike *Knowledge* it does not necessarily imply attention. There can be simple awareness without specific discrimination or recognition of the objective characteristics of the object, even though these characteristics must be deemed to have an effect.

The individual may not be able to verbalize the aspects of the stimulus which cause the awareness.[1]

It is difficult to find objectives which specify so low a level of reception since most teachers are concerned with obtaining and directing their students' attention at a higher level. A further difficulty is that "concern with a vague awareness on the part of the student" is difficult to verbalize as a specific behavioral objective. Description of the behavior in the very specific terms which make the behavior recognizable tends to define it at a higher level of attention giving. Thus, even the following objectives, which might be classified here, have to be read with the definition of simple awareness in mind, realizing that a teacher might so interpret them that they fall within or without the bounds of the category definition.

1.1 Awareness—Illustrative Educational Objectives

Develops awareness of aesthetic factors in dress, furnishings, architecture, city design, good art, and the like.

Observes with increasing differentiation the sights and sounds encountered in school and out.

Develops some consciousness of color, form, arrangement, and design in the objects and structures around him and in descriptive or symbolic representations of people, things, and situations.

Awareness of the importance of the prevention, early recognition, and treatment of marital discord and of behavior problems of children.

An awareness that there is an interdependence of nations in the creation and preservation of a satisfactory postwar world.

Recognition that there may be more than one acceptable point of view.

Awareness of the satisfactions that arise from good workmanship and integrity on the job.

Realization of the importance of nonvocational activities in a balanced adult life.

Sensitivity to social situations that are urgent.

Awareness of the feelings of others whose activities are of little interest to ourselves.

---

[1] In both the cognitive and affective domains consciousness is a major variable. However, in the cognitive domain it functions pretty much as a constant throughout. There is a high level of consciousness in cognitive activity at all stages of that *Handbook*. By contrast, in the affective domain consciousness builds up slowly to a high degree of specificity and then falls off in intensity as the process of internalization takes over.

1.1 Testing for Awareness

The essential behavior to be measured at the *Awareness* level is whether the student is conscious of something; whether he is aware of the existence of some person, phenomenon, event, or state of affairs. The notion of awareness carries with it a strong cognitive component. To be aware of something or of someone is certainly to know of it, even if the knowing is at the most superficial level conceivable.[1] During awareness the object or phenomenon stands out momentarily as a crude figure against a general background. Even when perceived clearly, the figure holds a peripheral rather than a central place in the student's psychological field because he has not yet invested it with importance. He simply notices the object or phenomenon, but without interest. In effect he says, "I am aware of it. But I couldn't care less about it."

It is important to note that a range of awarenesses can occur along a continuum from very unsophisticated or gross awareness to highly sophisticated and detailed awareness. In a class in art appreciation an example of gross awareness is simply being conscious of paintings, where such consciousness did not exist before. A more sophisticated awareness occurs when the teacher has succeeded in making the student conscious of the existence of different styles in painting. It is quite likely that some degree of internalization of the first awareness must take place before the second awareness can occur.

The major problem in testing for *Awareness* is to devise test situations which allow awareness to emerge without any direct hint from the examiner that the object or phenomenon exists. For example, suppose the art teacher is seeking to develop in the student an awareness of physical characteristics in a variety of art media (e.g., color, form, arrangement, and design). If the teacher then wanted to know whether such awareness had de-

[1] It is entirely possible for a person to be at the *Awareness* level in the affective domain and, at the same time, have a considerable amount of knowledge about the object or phenomenon. For example, an eleventh grader could possess a great deal of information about American history but could have absolutely no interest in this subject at all. His good performance on the cognitive examinations, in this case, would indicate that his affect has been invested in getting good grades rather than in an involvement in American history *per se*.

veloped, he certainly should not choose a test situation in which he presents art objects to the student and asks him to report whether or not he is aware of color, form, and other characteristics in them. Directing the student in the test situation to these characteristics makes him, by definition, aware of them.

A more reliable appraisal of this educational objective can be made by constructing less structured test situations. An example is to have the student look at a series of paintings, one at a time, and describe, within a specified short period of time, what he sees.[2] Should some of his descriptions be in terms of color, form, arrangement, and design, the teacher can infer that this student is aware of these characteristics. The relative number of allusions to the various characteristics can be taken as a measure of the relative strength of the characteristics of paintings in the student's awareness.

We cannot with certainty infer a lack of awareness if the student fails to mention these characteristics in his descriptions. It is entirely possible that he was aware of them when looking at the paintings but did not verbalize them. He even may have been aware of them at a semiconscious level. To determine whether this is the case the examiner would have to probe further with such a question as "Are there any other ways of describing this painting?" If, after a series of such questions, shading (for example) is still not mentioned by the student, the teacher can safely conclude that he is not aware of shading in paintings.

A more structured but less direct approach to testing for *Awareness* is illustrative test item *1.1–E*, of this section. Here the student is confronted with many paintings at once, which he is to arrange in pairs with similar artistic properties. Essentially this is a sorting and matching task. Awareness of color, for example, can be inferred if he uses this characteristic in establishing certain pairs. Should verbal descriptions of what the pairs have in common be required of the student, the examiner could develop a scoring scheme based not only on the number of times color was used to establish pairs, but also on qualitative aspects of color, such as hue and tone.

Illus. 1.1–A Sharp clues for a testing strategy can often be suggested by those *Awareness* objectives which are stated with a high degree of specificity. Consider, for example, this

[2]It goes without saying that the paintings used to elicit the awareness of particular characteristics must objectively possess these characteristics.

objective: "Awareness of the importance of the early recognition and treatment of behavior problems of children." One test situation which is directly suggested from this statement is to present the student with a series of comprehensive critical incidents of both normal and disturbed behaviors in the classroom, each of which requires teacher action. The student is instructed to read the behavioral incidents as though he were the teacher of these children. His task is to suggest what action he, as a teacher, should take in response to each critical incident. If the student prescribes for the most deviant incidents referral to the school psychologist or a talk with the child's parents concerning the advisability of professional help, he may be said to have the desired awareness. On the other hand, the student who suggests disciplinary measures for *both* normal and deviant behaviors is presumed not to possess the awareness in question.

Illus. 1.1–B A more structured form of this testing situation can be arranged by offering the student a list of five or six courses of action ranging in degree all the way from, let us say, "I would overlook this behavior" to "I would immediately refer the child to the school's psychological services office." After reading each incident the student is instructed to rank the various courses of action to be taken from "most desirable" to "least desirable." Appropriate procedures could be devised to give each student an *Awareness* score.

A more direct way of testing for *Awareness* is by means of simple information. Included in such a simple information test are only items which are defined as "easy" in terms of the age- and experience-level of the students being tested. The influence of both higher-order intellectual abilities and such other cognitive abilities as memory and inference should be kept to an absolute minimum in the response situation.

Illus. 1.1–C To illustrate what can be done to appraise *Awareness* through the use of simple information items, let us use an objective which is commonly found in the social-studies curriculum: "Awareness of the existence of the chief statesmen in international affairs." One way of testing for this awareness is to present the student with a set of photographs of Churchill, Johnson, Macmillan, De Gaulle, Erhard, Nasser, Khrushchev, Mao, Chiang, Castro, etc. In order to minimize the role of memory and knowledge, pictures should be limited to those figures that have been prominently featured in the press during the past year. The procedure would be to have the student write the name of the statesman underneath his photograph. The degree of *Awareness* would be proportional to the number of pictures identified correctly. More specific *Awareness* scores could be calculated on the basis of subpatterns of correct and incorrect responses.

Illus. 1.1-D Should photographs not be available or not be recognized by students, a variant procedure would be to have the student associate the name of the statesman with that of his country, either in a matching situation or, in order to reduce to a minimum the role of reasoning processes in the response, a "fill-in" situation such as:

Directions: On each line below fill in the blank space.

Statesman	*Nation*
Charles De Gaulle	______________
______________	Federal Republic of Germany (West Germany)
______________	Nationalist China (Formosa)
Nikita Khrushchev	______________
______________	Cuba
Mao-tse-Tung	______________
Gamal Abdel Nasser	______________
______________	Israel

This is a very simple test of information, and performance on it can be taken as a measure of *Awareness.* The nature of the information sought must be quite unsophisticated and straightforward, in terms (of course) of the student's level, and capable of having been received without conscious or purposive effort. Any student would have ample opportunity to learn this information if he attended to it. With regard to contemporary world statesmen, a tremendous amount of information is disseminated about them by all the mass communication media. Thus many of us, without even being willing to receive it, are aware of some of the more general characteristics of the international scene. One does not have to be knowledgeable in current affairs to be aware of who is currently Prime Minister of Great Britain and who is presently directing the destiny of the Soviet Union.

For those examiners who would not want to accept the idea of making inferences about *Awareness* from tests of simple information, a technique of the free-association type would probably be more acceptable. Here the student is instructed to write next to each statesman's name any phrase or sentence which is suggested to him by that name. The responses obtained can be scored in terms of both the existence of an awareness and the depth of it.

1.1 Awareness—Selected Examples from the Test Literature

Illus. 1.1–E *Objective*: Consciousness of color, form, arrangement, and design in paintings.

Test: *Finding Pairs of Pictures.* Eight-Year Study, Progressive Education Association. Cited in Chester W. Harris, Bruno Bettelheim, and Paul B. Diederich, "Aspects of Appreciation." In E. R. Smith and R. W. Tyler, *Appraising and Recording Student Progress* (New York: Harper and Brothers, 1942, pp. 276–307).

This instrument consists of a sheet of cardboard "approximately 24″ × 44″ in size, on which 40 colored postcards are mounted. These are copies of more or less well-known paintings ranging in periods represented from the Italian and German Renaissance to modern and contemporary art. Dutch, Spanish XVIIth century, and French XIXth century paintings are included. Portraits, landscapes, and still-lifes are represented. . . . No titles or names of artists are given, but each painting is marked with a number of identification."

From the 40 stimulus pictures the student is instructed to select pairs of pictures "which have important artistic features in common" such as colors, design, mood, and so forth. He is warned against making major use of similarity of subject matter in his pairings. No limits are set as to how often a particular picture is to be paired. The student is instructed to find, if possible, at least 20, but not more than 30, pairs of pictures. He notes the pairs on an answer sheet with the following format:

1. No. ________ and No. ________ make a pair.
2. No. ________ and No. ________ make a pair.

Through the cognitive act of producing what he deems to be similar pairs of paintings, the student without any previous experience with such art objects becomes conscious of certain of their characteristics for the first time. He may not be able to verbalize these characteristics. At the *Awareness* level we are simply interested in knowing what he is attending to in these pictures. Thus the criterion for determining *Awareness* is his ability to note pairs of similar pictures. Knowing whether he can identify the names of the paintings and their artists and periods or whether he has derived satisfaction in the viewing are matters which need not be considered if one is only appraising at the *Awareness* level.

Illus. 1.1-F *Objective*: Awareness of the works of famous musical composers.[3]

Test: *Test of Educational Progress in Music, Art, and Literature* (Chicago: Study of Educational Progress, University of Chicago, 1946, p. 7).

Directions: Blacken answer space T if the statement is true; F if it is false. Do not guess blindly. A statement must be true in all its parts to be marked *true*.

42. One of Bach's most celebrated compositions is the symphonic poem, "Death and Transfiguration." (F)[4]
47. Haydn was outstanding in the composition of string quartets and symphonies. (T)
48. Mozart's string quartets are more nearly like Haydn's than like the later Beethoven quartets. (T)
49. Mozart composed every type of music except opera. (F)
50. Schubert was outstanding in the composition of songs. (T)
57. Verdi wrote *Aïda, Rigoletto, La Traviata,* and *Carmen.* (F)

Illus. 1.1-G *Objective*: Awareness of works in literature.

Test: *General Acquaintance Test in Literature* (Chicago: Board of Examinations, University of Chicago, 1952).

Directions: The items in this test are arranged in sets of *three*, with five possible responses printed to the right of each group. For each item, blacken your Answer Sheet with the letter corresponding to the response that best completes the statement begun on the left. In no case will the same response be correct for more than one item within a single group of three. There is no objection to careful and intelligent guessing here.

271. In *Man and Superman* by Shaw (D)	A—the hero's father has been executed.
272. In *The Emperor Jones* by O'Neill (B)	B—the hero had been a Pullman porter.
273. In *Winterset* by Anderson (A)	C—the hero is a white ruler of a South Sea island.
	D—the hero finally becomes engaged to the heroine.
	E—the hero is finally hanged.

[3]The items of this illustration and of illustration *1.1-G* are measuring a rather sophisticated level of *Awareness*.

[4]The response alternative which contributes to the *Affective Taxonomy* subcategory score is printed in parentheses after each item.

274. In *The Inferno* by Dante (B)	A—the hero is accompanied by the devil.
275. In *Don Quixote* by Cervantes (D)	B—the hero is accompanied by a poet.
276. In *Faust* by Goethe (A)	C—the hero is accompanied by his father.
	D—the hero is accompanied by a servant.
	E—the hero is accompanied by an ambitious woman.

1.2 Willingness to Receive

In this category we have come a step up the ladder but are still dealing with what appears to be cognitive behavior. At a minimum level we are here describing the behavior of being willing to tolerate a given stimulus, not to avoid it. Like *Awareness,* it involves a neutrality or suspended judgment toward the stimulus. This is a frequent objective of teachers of the arts, since we are prone to reject and avoid some of the newer art forms. Dissonant music and modernistic art, to name two, would be examples toward which an art teacher might seek a willingness to attend. At this level of the continuum the teacher is not concerned that the student seek it out, nor even, perhaps, that in an environment crowded with many other stimuli the learner will necessarily attend to the stimulus. Rather, at worst, given the opportunity to attend in a field with relatively few competing stimuli, the learner is not actively seeking to avoid it. At best, he is willing to take notice of the phenomenon and give it his attention.

Mock-ups, or the presentation of the phenomenon in a purposely simplified form, will quite frequently be used here to help the learner isolate the phenomenon. Animation, cutaways, graphs, charts, and other audiovisual devices are useful for this purpose. Or the teacher may create an environment in which there are few competing stimuli in the physical surrounding; an example of such a method is the use of individual soundproof booths for listening to musical recordings.

Some of the terms found in objectives which are likely to be classified in this category are: amenable to, disposed toward, inclined toward, tractable with respect to, etc.

1.2 Willingness to Receive—Illustrative Educational Objectives

Develops a tolerance for a variety of types of music.

Accepts differences of race and culture, among people known.

Accepts as associates and cohelpers, in everyday undertakings, other human beings without regard to race, religion, or national origin.

Attends (carefully) when others speak—in direct conversation, on the telephone, in audiences.

Listens to others with respect.

Appreciation (tolerance) of cultural patterns exhibited by individuals from other groups—religious, social, political, economic, national, etc.

Appreciation (recognition) of family members as persons with needs and interests of their own.

Increase in sensitivity to human need and pressing social problems.

1.2 Testing for Willingness to Receive

In testing at the *Willingness to receive* level of the *Affective Taxonomy* it is assumed that awareness of the stimulus has already been achieved. Now that awarenesses do exist the measurement task at the 1.2 level is essentially negative rather than positive: to determine whether there is an absence of a rejection of the stimulus. We are not quite ready to say that the student is interested in the stimulus in the sense that he is drawn to it or finds something attractive in it. He has yet to invest it with a positive valence, but he does not reject it. If there is a positive aspect to his perception of the stimulus, it can best be described as having a tolerance for it.

The general appraisal model at this level is to be found in the traditional interest inventory. Here the student is presented with a series of stimuli in the form of activities to perform (e.g., visit an art museum, read a biography of Michelangelo) or in the form of a series of questions to discuss or consider (e.g., What is Gothic architecture? Who are the leading contemporary composers?). His task is to examine each item and to indicate, by choosing one of several response alternatives, whether or not he would like to perform the activity or discuss the question in class. The three-alternative Like-Indifferent-Dislike response model is the one most commonly used. Five response alternatives are employed in some instruments, but this is the exception rather than the rule. The two alternatives added represent very strong dispositions, one toward the stimulus and the other away from it.

The key to using interest-type items at the *Willingness to receive* level is the way in which response alternatives are phrased. It is preferable to omit response alternatives which imply a strong positive affect, such as "The question is very interesting." The term "very interesting" suggests a positive attraction which the *Willingness to receive* level does not possess. We come closer to appraising this level of the *Affective Taxonomy* if the student selects alternatives which contain neutral or tentatively positive words like "possibly," "uncertain," "indifferent," "interesting."

Just as there are different levels of *Awareness* of the same phenomenon or object, so there are also different levels of *Willingness to receive*. This is the depth dimension of the category. One student may be willing to visit the local art museum but may reject the suggestion that he visit it for the express purpose of seeing the collection of French impressionist paintings. Another student may be not only amenable to both activities but even disposed toward visiting the French impressionist gallery at a particular time of day when the natural light makes for more appropriate viewing. It is entirely possible to include in one instrument these and other items tapping the same dimension in order to obtain a measure of depth of the willingness of the student to view paintings at the art museum.

Another dimension of *Willingness to receive* which is operative and can be appraised is that of breadth. This dimension refers to an amenability to a large variety of related activities. For example, in an art course breadth would be represented by a willingness to read about art, to view art, and to develop skills in several art media.

A willingness to receive a stimulus does not necessarily imply the achievement of some degree of mastery of it. It does imply, as pointed out above, that the student is sufficiently aware of the nature of the stimulus that he can make the judgment required at the 1.2 level. Should the typical American high-school student be confronted, in a sports-and-games *Willingness to receive* instrument, with the question, "Would you like to play cricket?", he would know that cricket is an English game. But in order to decide whether he would be disposed toward playing this game he would have to know something more specific about it. Thus in constructing instruments at this level provision must be made to allow the student lacking sufficient awareness to indicate this fact. One can either have an additional response category for this condition or instruct him not to respond to those items he knows so little about that he cannot really determine how he would be disposed toward them.

1.2 Willingness to Receive—Selected Examples from the Test Literature

Illus. 1.2–A *Objective*: Disposition toward considering basic health questions.

Test: Adapted from *Health Interests; Inventory 1.3* (Chicago: Cooperative Study in General Education, American Council on Education, 1941).

Directions: Your school wants to determine the kinds of health problems which you would be willing to consider in class. Examine each question in this booklet. To the left of each question number there are four letters.

Encircle letter *A* if you are willing to consider the question in school.
Encircle letter *B* if you are willing to consider the question but you think it should not be dealt with in school.[5]
Encircle letter *C* if you don't care whether the question is considered or not, in school or away from school.
Encircle letter *D* if you are ***not*** willing to consider the question because it holds no interest for you.

2. Are pimples caused by poor digestion?
4. What is the proper treatment for boils?
13. What is the cause of loss of hair in a young man?
14. Can dandruff be removed permanently?
28. Is the skipping of meals injurious to one's health?
102. Is a coat of tan healthy?
123. When should children be told about reproduction?

Scoring rationale: Response alternatives *A, B,* and *C* fall within the meaning of the 1.2 level. Alternative *C* reflects an indifference rather than a rejection. Alternative *D* is the only one which clearly indicates an unwillingness to receive. In terms of the objective of this illustration a student's *Willingness to receive* is inferred on the basis of the total number of *A* and *B* responses that he makes.

Illus. 1.2–B *Objective*: Interest in voluntary reading.

Test: Adapted from *Questionnaire on Voluntary Reading; Test 3.32* (Chicago: Evaluation in the Eight-Year Study, Progressive Education Association, 1940).

---

[5]This response alternative is included for the benefit of those students who would object to the consideration of the question in school on moral or religious grounds or both.

Directions: The purpose of this questionnaire is to discover what you really think about the reading which you do in your leisure time. . . . Consider each question carefully and answer it as *honestly* and as *frankly* as you possibly can. . . . There are three ways to mark the Answer Sheet:

Y means that your answer to the question is *Yes.*
U means that your answer to the question is *Uncertain.*
N means that your answer to the question is *No.*

1. Do you wish that you had more time to devote to reading? (*Y*)
28. Do you have in mind one or two books which you would like to read sometime soon? (*Y*)
41. Is it usually impossible for you to read for as long as an hour without becoming bored? (*N*)
68. Are there any well-known works of English or American literature which you would like to read during your leisure time? (*Y*)

Scoring rationale: The letters in the parentheses which follow the questions indicate the responses keyed for *Willingness to receive.* Each question in this illustration contains an intimation of a very tentative and general disposition toward voluntary reading which is the essence of the 1.2 level of the *Affective Taxonomy.* Should a student respond in the keyed direction to question 1, such a response does not necessarily mean that he is an avid and committed reader. It can only be interpreted to mean that he is favorably disposed to read more if there is more time available to devote to it.

Illus. 1.2–C *Objective*: Willingness to take part in musical activities.

Test: Adapted from *Interest Index; Test 8.2a* (Chicago: Evaluation in the Eight-Year Study, Progressive Education Association, 1939).

Directions: As you read each item below underline *one* of the three letters after the number of that item on the Answer Sheet.

Underline *L* if you *would like* to do what the item says.
Underline *I* if you *neither like nor dislike* what the items says but you would still be willing to do it.
Underline *D* if you dislike what the item says and would not want to do it.

12. Sing songs at parties, picnics, etc.
15. Sing in a glee club, chorus, or choir.
62. Play in an orchestra or band.
65. Make up tunes to hum, or compose music.

Scoring rationale: Both *L* and *I* responses are keyed as indicating *Willingness to receive.*

Illus. 1.2–D *Objective*: Amenable toward learning a foreign language.

Test: Adapted from *Interest Index; Test 8.2a* (see illustration *1.2–C*).

Directions: The purpose of this questionnaire is to discover what you really think about the activities that you engage in in your leisure time. . . . Consider each question carefully and answer it as *honestly* and as *frankly* as you can. . . . There are three ways to mark the Answer Sheet.

> *Y* means that your answer to the question is *Yes*.
> *U* means that your answer to the question is *Uncertain*.
> *N* means that your answer to the question is *No*.

6. Correspond in a foreign language with a student in another country. (*Y*)
34. Listen to broadcasts in a foreign language. (*Y*)
56. Make English translations of passages written in a foreign language. (*Y*)
81. Compare the different ways in which the same idea is expressed in English and in foreign languages. (*Y*)
84. Study how English words are derived from words in other languages. (*Y*)

1.3 Controlled or Selected Attention

At a somewhat higher level we are concerned with a new phenomenon, the differentiation of a given stimulus into figure and ground at a conscious or perhaps semiconscious level—the differentiation of aspects of a stimulus which is perceived as clearly marked off from adjacent impressions. The perception is still without tension or assessment, and the student may not know the technical terms or symbols with which to describe it correctly or precisely to others. Like the training of Rudyard Kipling's Kim to play the great game of a spy, this may be a training of the eyes or other sensory faculties to a keener awareness of what has been sensorily received all along.

Such training is exemplified in the efforts of the home-economics teacher to make her students aware of aesthetic design in dresses. She hopes that when they have become aware of these principles in dresses, they will also see them in furnishings, architecture, city design, etc. She is concerned at this level that they be consciously or semiconsciously aware of these design factors.

In other instances this may refer not so much to the selectivity of attention as to the control of attention, so that when certain stimuli are present they will be attended to. The social-studies teacher is concerned with impressing his students not only with the alert perception of the economic needs of a portion of our society, but with the active attention to these needs when they occur in the immediate vicinity of the learner. The music teacher is concerned that the student be aware of the background music and the mood it sets when viewing a dramatic film.

In contrast to the previous level, there is an element here of the learner's controlling the attention, so that the favored stimulus is selected and attended to despite competing and distracting stimuli.

1.3 Controlled or Selected Attention—Illustrative Educational Objectives

Listens to music with some discrimination as to its mood and meaning and with some recognition of the contributions of various musical elements and instruments to the total effect.

Listens for rhythm in poetry or prose read aloud.

Sensitive to the importance of keeping informed on current political and social matters.

Alertness toward different types of voluntary reading.

Listens carefully for and remembers names of persons to whom he is introduced.

Appreciation of the contribution of the arts toward man's seeking of the good life.

Listens for picturesque words in stories read aloud or told.

Preference for newspaper readings.

Alertness toward human values and judgments on life as they are recorded in literature.

1.3 Testing for Controlled or Selected Attention

The general willingness to receive which exists at the 1.2 level has now taken on a more specific and precise form. In a word, the stimulus is more clearly and consciously perceived, the student being more intently aware of it. The very strength of the awareness inevitably adds a strong cognitive component to the perception, which is reflected by such descriptive terms as "favors it," "prefers it." At level 1.2 the student reports that, at worst, he is not averse to singing in the school glee club and, at best, he is willing to try this activity. At level 1.3 this activity moves closer to the center of the awareness stage and quite often is in the spotlight. When asked to rank a variety of activities according to preference, he ranks singing in the glee club high on the list.

The interest-inventory model can be used for appraising at this level of awareness as well as at the previous level (1.2). In general, the activities and questions remain the same, but the response alternatives keyed for controlled or selected attention are constructed in order to reflect the greater amount of attention to the stimulus. Examples of such responses are: "I have a strong intention to take up this activity." "This matter intrigues me."

A second measurement strategy is not to change the response alternatives but to increase the specificity of the item. Consider this question: "Do you wish that you had more time to devote to reading?" This is an item which reflects a general and somewhat vague intention to do something. It is classified as a 1.2 *Willingness to receive* item if the response to it is "Yes." But transform this item to "Are you keeping a list of books which you plan to read during the next few months?" Here the attention is much clearer and more explicit. Therefore, if the answer is still in the affirmative, this item is classified as *Selected attention.*

The forced-choice method enables the examiner to test for selected awareness. In this method the examiner chooses a variety of different activities or tasks and presents them to the student as pairs in all their possible combinations. The student indicates which member of each pair he prefers. Since each activity is paired with every other one, the pattern of preferences is the basis for determining whether there is any differential selection and, if so, which activity or activities have been selected.

In many parts of the curriculum, evidence of the attainment of *Controlled or selected attention* can be obtained by means of simple skill tests. The model for this type of approach is the test for following directions or the listening-comprehension test modified to record and analyze what the student attends to rather than what he comprehends. Variations of this test model can also be constructed.

Illus. 1.3–A For example, suppose the literature teacher has the objective "Listen for picturesque words in stories read aloud or told." To test whether he has succeeded in developing such attention he might, after reading a story to his class, present it with a list of the story's picturesque words embedded among picturesque words which did not appear in the story. The task for the students is to identify those words which appeared in the story heard. Evidence of selective attending is inferred if the student makes correct identifications.

Illus. 1.3–B As an alternate method of testing in this situation, picturesque words not used in the story are selected and embedded among nonpicturesque words, the goal of the examiner being to see whether the student can identify the former.

It is preferable to test for selected awareness at the time it is expected to occur. The advantage of such an approach is the elimination of recall as a contaminating factor in attention. A variety of stimuli is presented in the situation. The student notes his awareness at the time it occurs. He does this by constructing lists of, or writing short essays on, what is perceived. The analysis of the student's productions attempts to draw a profile of the stimuli presented in terms of which ones are focused upon and which are not attended to at all.

1.3 Controlled or Selected Attention—Selected Examples from the Test Literature

Illus. 1.3–C *Objective*: Alertness toward different types of voluntary reading.

Test: *Questionnaire on Voluntary Reading; Test 3.32* (Chicago: Evaluation in the Eight-Year Study, Progressive Education Association, 1940).

Directions: The purpose of this questionnaire is to discover what you really think about the reading which you do in your leisure time. . . . There are three ways to mark the Answer Sheet:

Y means that your answer to the question is *Yes*.
U means that your answer to the question is *Uncertain*.
N means that your answer to the question is *No*.

15. Would you like to know much more about the history and development of some type of literature, such as the drama or short story? (*Y*)
40. Are you interested in knowing more about literary awards, such as the Pulitzer prizes and the Nobel prizes? (*Y*)
42. Is there any type of nonfiction, such as biography, travel, or science, which you would like to read more of at present? (*Y*)

Illus. 1.3–D *Objective*: Sensitive to the importance of keeping informed on current political and social matters.

Test: *Interest Index; Test 8.2* (Chicago: Evaluation in the Eight-Year Study, Progressive Education Association, 1939).

Directions: As you read each item below underline *one* of the three letters after the number of that item on the Answer Sheet:

Underline *L* (like) if you like or want to do what the item says.
Underline *I* (indifferent) if you neither like nor dislike what the item says.
Underline *D* (dislike) if you dislike it or would not enjoy doing it.

28. To analyze, compare, and criticize the platforms or proposals of different political parties. (*L*)
53. To hear lectures or radio talks on political and social problems. (*L*)
83. To follow day-by-day reports of the development of some national or international situation or problem. (*L*)
103. To read detailed accounts by foreign correspondents of the background and causes of events in other countries. (*L*)

Illus. 1.3–E *Objective*: Preference for newspaper reading.

Test: *Questionnaire on Newspaper Reading; Form 327* (Chicago: Evaluation in the Eight-Year Study, Progressive Education Association, no date).

5. I read the following sections. (Mark *U* if you usually read the section, *O* if you read it occasionally, and *R* if you read it rarely):

a. News ______	i. Art notes ______
b. Editorials ______	j. Sports ______
c. Financial ______	k. Society ______
d. Funnies ______	l. Stories ______
e. Magazine ______	m. Ads ______
f. Book reviews ______	n. TV and radio ______
g. Theatre notes ______	o. Others (specify) ______
h. Music notes ______	______

Scoring rationale: Regular reading of a section of a newspaper is evidence of *Selected Attention*. Occasional reading can be taken as evidence of a *Willingness to receive,* whereas rare reading of a section suggests momentary awareness, possibly produced by a compelling headline or photograph or by a friend's suggestion to read.

Illus. 1.3–F *Objective*: Appreciation of the contribution of the arts toward man's seeking of the good life.

Test: *Inventory of the Arts* (Chicago: Cooperative Study in General Education, American Council on Education, no date).

Directions: In this inventory you are asked to express some of your reactions to the arts. . . . Read each statement carefully. Then indicate your reactions on the Answer Sheet by underlining one of the three letters after the number of that item. Underline:

A if you feel that this statement is a fairly adequate expression of your general opinion.

U if you are uncertain whether you agree or disagree with the opinion expressed in this statement.
D if you disagree with the opinion expressed in the statement.

11. Everybody can appreciate art, and for this purpose it is not necessary to know a lot about art.[6] (*D*)
26. The artist, the musician, and the poet have no great or no immediate influence on our daily life. (*D*)
29. The spirit of a period is best expressed in its arts. (*A*)
44. One of the most important purposes of art is to make you more aware of social problems you were not conscious of before. (*A*)

[6]For a response to be made in the keyed direction for this item as well as for item 29, it is probably necessary that a high cognitive level have been attained by the respondent.

2.0 RESPONDING

At this level we are concerned with responses which go beyond merely attending to the phenomenon. The student is sufficiently motivated that he is not just willing to attend, but perhaps it is correct to say that he is actively attending. As a first stage in a "learning by doing" process the student is committing himself in some small measure to the phenomenon involved. This is a very low level of commitment, and we would not say at this level that this was "a value of his" or that he had "such and such an attitude." These terms belong to the next higher level that we describe. But we could say that he is doing something with or about the phenomenon besides merely perceiving it, as would be true at the level immediately below this of 1.3 *Controlled or Selected Attention*. An example of such responding would be the compliance with rules of good health or safety or obedience to any of a number of rules of conduct.

This category of *Responding* has been divided into three subcategories to illustrate the continuum of responding as the learner becomes more fully committed to the practice or phenomena of the objective. The lowest stage is illustrated in the preceding paragraph and is named 2.1 *Acquiescence in responding*. As the name implies, there is the element of compliance or obedience at this level which distinguishes it from the next level, that of 2.2 *Willingness to respond*. Finally, at a still higher level of internalization, there is found a 2.3 *Satisfaction in response* not reached at the previous level of willingness or assent to respond. When there is an emotional response of pleasure, zest, or enjoyment, we have reached this third level.

This description of the latter two subcategories makes still clearer the "learning by doing" aspect of this category—the increasing depth of internalization as the learner takes more and more responsibility for initiating action. For example, the teacher, in seeking the attainment of one of these objectives, so sets the classroom scene that the student finds himself joining with zest in group singing.

This is the category that many teachers will find best describes their "interest" objectives. Most commonly we use the term to indicate the desire that a child become sufficiently involved in or committed to a subject, phenomenon, or activity that he will seek it out and gain satisfaction from working with it or engaging in it. But since the term "interest" has a variety of meanings, it is hoped that the teacher finds that classifying an objective here, or at another level in the scheme, lends a precision that is now lacking in current use of the word.

There is some question as to where the third subcategory is best located to be an integral part of the hierachy. Should it be where it is now? Or should it be between the first and second categories of 2.0 *Responding*? In order to establish the clearest hierarchy, 2.3 *Satisfaction in response* has been placed after 2.2 *Willingness to respond* on the grounds that in most instances a response is not likely to produce satisfaction unless willingness has already been established. This problem is further discussed in the 2.3 category description.

2.1 Acquiescence in Responding

At this level we are concerned with what might be thought of as the first level of active responding after the learner has given his attention. We might use the word "obedience" or "compliance" to describe the behavior. As both of these terms indicate, there is a passiveness so far as the initiation of the behavior is concerned, and the stimulus calling for this behavior is not subtle. Compliance is perhaps a better term than obedience, since there is more of the element of reaction to a suggestion and less of the implication of resistance or yielding unwillingly.

In 2.1 *Acquiescence in responding* the student makes the response, but he has not fully accepted the necessity for doing so. There is the implication here that, should the conditions be such that other alternatives of response were open, and were there no pressures to conform with the teacher-held standard or social norm, the student might well choose an alternative response.

Few objectives will be found which specify this level of behavior. Although the achievement of compliant or obedient behavior in the school is a frequent outcome, rarely does it appear in the objectives of the school. Objectives state the ideal goals of learning. Obedience and compliance are hardly ideal goals. In fact, unlike the other levels of behavior, which may be thought of as steps toward self-motivated and self-directed behavior, behavior instilled in the learner at this level may never become more internalized and more self-directed. Often the consequence is the blocking of further progress up the continuum except under sustained external influence. Responding in an acquiescent manner may have the same external manifestations as internalized behavior, but the internal aspects of the behavior are quite different.

It is rare, therefore, that one finds objectives which describe this level of behavior. The major areas in which we find objectives at this level are those of health and safety, where the danger that harm may come to the student as a result of the ignorance of, or noncompliance with, the rules outweighs the desirability that he internalize this behavior at a higher level from the outset.

2.1 Acquiescence in Responding—Illustrative Educational Objectives[1]

Willingness to force oneself to participate with others.

Willingness to comply with health regulations.

Completes his homework.

Observes the traffic rules on foot, on a bicycle, or on another conveyance at intersections and elsewhere.

Visits museums when told to do so.

Reads the assigned literature.

Obeys the playground regulations.

2.1 Testing for Acquiescence in Responding[2]

The key behaviors at this level are acquiescence and compliance. Although there are few educational objectives which specify this level of behavior, there are many instances of the

---

[1] Educational objectives classified at the 2.1 level are of two types: (*a*) *Unstated but implied objectives.* Since co-operation or acquiescence of the child is necessary to ongoing instructional activity, there is a whole group of unspecified 2.1 objectives calling for normally expected behaviors. Examples are: performing assigned homework, purchasing a ticket to the student concert when told to do so, etc. (*b*) *Overtly stated objectives.* These are likely to describe behavior less clearly falling into the normal pattern of acquiescence for the age. For example: observing the ordinances regarding bicycles, such as having inspection once a year by the police. Objectives of the first kind are likely to be assumed as part of getting along in school. Objectives of the second kind are more likely to be a conscious and integral part of the instructional effort.

[2] Acquiescence is a built-in characteristic of test situations at all levels of the affective domain. But at the 2.1 level we must be careful at all times to distinguish between acquiescence with respect to behavior related to the educational objective and acquiescence in the sense that the very fact that the student is willing to take the test is an attempt to please or to avoid displeasure.

exhibition of such behaviors. If it is to function effectively, the instructional effort demands much compliant behavior. Whether the student wants to or not, he is required to exhibit a variety of behaviors—to complete prescribed homework assignments, observe traffic regulations, visit the dentist annually for an examination, and so forth. Of course, the teacher strives to reduce the incidence of acquiescent behavior to an absolute minimum.

Securing evidence as to whether or not the student has made the desired response is the major task of testing at this level. The basic question for testing, then, is: Is the student actually responding? That is, does he observe the traffic rules on his way to school? Does he read a book during his lecture time? Does he visit the dentist periodically for an examination? These responses can be recorded by direct observation or by asking the student outright.

We can say, for those students who are making a particular response, that at the very minimum they are acquiescing. It is quite possible that some are responding at a higher level of the *Affective Taxonomy*.

Should the examiner wish to find out whether the response was self-initiated or was made essentially at the request of another person—be it teacher, parent, sibling, friend, or adult model—relevant evidence can be collected by asking the student to state the reason for his response, either in a free-response manner or by having him choose the one of several response alternatives which comes closest to explaining the source of the motivation for responding. The examiner should use this direct approach only when he is certain that the respondent will not attempt to deny acquiescent responding because he feels that this type of response, if known to his teacher, will produce social disapproval and punishment.

There are several other methods for determining whether an observed or recorded response is self-initiated or otherwise. Take, for example, the observation of traffic rules en route to school. The vast majority of students obey them during school hours. Yet we cannot say that all who obey them do so willingly. To determine who are merely complying with these rules, the examiner can devise a questionnaire for parents which asks about their child's traffic behavior in a number of standard situations away from school. Or the examiner can make systematic observations of students going to school on, let us say, a Saturday morning when they are gathering for a special trip to the museum. The enforcers of the school traffic regulations, the crossing guards and the policemen, are not on duty. The children know this, and those who disobey the traffic regulations on that Saturday can be said to be the ones who merely comply with the regulations on school days.

The displaying of certain types of behavior in class can be taken by the examiner as evidence of acquiescence. Participation with little interest or enthusiasm in, for example, a class discussion or in what the student is doing alone may sometimes be evidence of acquiescent behavior. Such evidence must be interpreted with caution, since there might be many causes of lack of enthusiasm. Daydreaming, however, or doing something other than what is required at the moment, indicates lack of acquiescence.

More direct evidence of acquiescent behavior can be secured by noting which students in a given situation respond only when continuously reminded to do so. The more often a student must be told to do something, the more acquiescent is his response, if any.

The concrete products of a student's learning effort can be examined in a variety of ways for acquiescent responding. Typical evidences of 2.1 behavior in written assignments, oral presentations, book reports, term papers, and examination booklets are the exertion of the very least amount of effort in order to get by, the literal following of requirements, and a listless or unenthusiastic presentation.

Acquiescent behavior may be indicated when a sloppily executed report stands out against a series of previously completed neat reports. This can be taken to mean that either there has been a regression in affect—that is, the student has lost his lively interest in the subject—or the student does not like the topic being studied.

Activities check lists or inventories of the type mentioned at the 1.2 and 1.3 levels can be used as tests at this level. Whereas at the *Receiving* levels, activities can be used which the student is merely aware of, at the *Responding* levels the activities have to be limited to those which the student has actually experienced. *Acquiescence in responding* is indicated when the student chooses such response alternatives as "I don't like to do it," "Doing it bores me," "I only do it when I have to," "I only do it when a friend suggests it."

It is difficult to mask the intention of a check list or inventory. Here again the examiner is concerned with obtaining valid responses. To circumvent this problem he may devise projective-type tests.

Illus. 2.1–A An example of such an instrument in, let us say, appreciation of reading is to construct a series of situations involving books, libraries, bookstores, and so forth. Each situation is a picture of two students, one involved in some activity that is associated with reading, such as reading at night in one's room, standing outside a bookstore, or having books charged out at the library. The second student is depicted as saying something to the first one. The task for the respondent is to supply, as quickly as possible, what the second student in the picture is saying to the first. Evidence of acquiescent responding is obtained if his responses contain such remarks as: "Don't waste your time reading tonight, if you are up on your homework." "I never borrow a book that isn't assigned by a teacher." "I buy only the books that are required."

2.1 Acquiescence in Responding—Selected Examples from the Test Literature

Illus. 2.1–B *Objective*: Willingness to comply with health regulations.

Test: Adapted from *Health Activities; Inventory 1.1* (Chicago: Cooperative Study in General Education, American Council on Education, 1941).

Directions: For each activity listed below:

1. Mark an X in *Column 1* if you perform the activity *without being told or reminded to do it.*
2. Mark an X in *Column 2* if you perform the activity *only when told or reminded to do it.*
3. Mark an X in *Column 3* if you *do not perform the activity.*

	Column 1	Column 2	Column 3
12. Visit a dentist annually.	_____	_____	_____
15. Wear overshoes or rubbers during wet, cold weather.	_____	_____	_____
52. Go to bed about the same time each night.	_____	_____	_____

Scoring rationale: Responses entered in Column 2 are keyed as 2.1 responses.

Illus. 2.1–C *Objective*: Willingness to comply with sound health practices.

Test: Adapted from *Health Activities; Inventory 1.1* (See illustration *2.1–B*).

Directions: Answer each question listed below by marking an X in either the YES or the NO columns.

69. Do you call a doctor only when you are sick enough to go to bed? (Y)
70. Do you put off or avoid going to a dentist as long as possible? (Y)

Illus. 2.1–D[3] *Objective*: Increased appetite and taste for what is good in literature.

Test: Adapted from *Questionnaire on Voluntary Reading; Test 3.32* (Chicago: Evaluation in the Eight-Year Study, Progressive Education Association, 1940).

Directions: The purpose of this questionnaire is to discover what you really think about the reading which you do in your leisure time.... Consider each question carefully and answer it as *honestly* and as *frankly* as you possibly can. There are no "right" answers as such. It is not expected that your own thoughts or feelings or activities relating to books should be like those of anyone else. There are three ways to mark the Answer Sheet:

Y means that your answer to the question is *Yes.*
U means that your answer to the question is *Uncertain.*
N means that your answer to the question is *No.*

30. Do you ever read essays, apart from school requirements? (*N*)
53. Do you ordinarily read fewer books during the summer vacation period than you do during a similar period of time while school is in session? (*Y*)
55. Have you ever done further reading or consulted other people in an attempt to learn more about the period, the events, or the places presented in a book which you have read? (*N*)
67. Do you read books chiefly because your parents or teachers urge you to do so? (*Y*)

2.2 Willingness to Respond

The key to this level is in the term "willingness," with its implication of capacity for voluntary activity. This is not so much a

[3]Although the items in this illustration are keyed for 2.1, the objective, as stated, is not a 2.1 objective. In fact, it is classified as 3.1 *Acceptance of a value.* Educational objectives in reading are rarely, if ever, stated at the 2.1 level. However, if an objective were to be stated at this level, it would take a form similar to "Completion of assigned readings."

response to outside prompting as it is a voluntary response from choice. English and English (1958, p. 122) suggest that the term "co-operation," which is one that fits in this category, is a euphemism for obedience. While this is clearly true in some school uses, in general when the term "co-operation" is used in school objectives there is the implication that the learner is sufficiently commited to exhibiting the behavior that he does so, not just out of a fear of punishment, but "on his own" or voluntarily. It may help to note that the element of resistance or of yielding unwillingly, which is possibly present at the previous level, is here replaced with consent or proceeding from one's own choice.

This is an important category for education, and one can find a large number of objectives which fit it. The behavior specified does not indicate how willingness to behave in this manner is attained, whether by telling the reasons, by positively reinforcing the behavior so that the reward in itself becomes a reason for so acting, or in other ways. Many of the objectives categorized at this level are socially desirable ones which, upon being exhibited, bring social approval to the learner and so are "self-reinforcing." In this sense the teacher's task is often reduced to that of so setting the environment that the behavior is emitted in a social situation. This is probably the dominant means of attaining many of the social objectives here classified.

2.2 Willingness to Respond—Illustrative Educational Objectives

Voluntarily looks for informational books dealing with hobbies or other topics in which he is interested.

Voluntarily reads magazines and newspapers designed for young children.

Voluntarily seeks new information about his physical environment—the weather, the sky, the earth, living things, and machines, including the mechanical means of transportation and communication.

Engages on his own in a variety of constructive hobbies and recreational activities.

Displays an interest in actively participating in research projects.

Practices the rules of good health, particularly with reference to rest, food, and sanitation.

Practices the rules of safety—in the school, on the playground, on the street, and in the home.

Practices the rules of conservation—protecting needed plant and animal life, avoiding waste of essential materials, etc.

Responds with consistent, active, and deep interest to intellectual stimuli.

Performs simple experiments relating to biological or physical science (to satisfy his curiosity about scientific questions).

Assumes full responsibility for his duties as a member of a family.

Co-operates in worthy enterprises undertaken by groups of which he is a member.

Keeps still when the occasion or the situation *calls* for silence.

Contributes to group discussion by asking thought-provoking questions or supplying relevant information and ideas.

Willingness to be of service to the group of which he is a member.

Voluntarily reads about the life and work of great artists and composers.

Interest in reading as a source of information on human behavior.

Co-operates in the production of a room or school newspaper or magazine.

Asks pertinent questions in discussion when the topic interests him.

Assumes responsibility for helping to make discussions successful.

Interests himself in social problems broader than those of the local community.

Has a scientific interest exhibited through reading, making collections, conducting experiments, or going on excursions.

Acquaints himself with significant current issues in international, political, social, and economic affairs through voluntary reading and discussion.

Considers the convenience of others in using the telephone.

Participates actively and thoughtfully in group discussion, with growing "awareness of audience."

Reads widely so as to extend and enrich experience.

Acceptance of responsibility for his own health and for the protection of the health of others.

Has continuing interest in reading books and periodicals that bear upon present-day personal and social problems and experiences.

Sense of responsibility for participating in desirable community activities.

Acceptance of primary responsibility for making major life choices.

Acceptance of the desirability of exploration and tentative choice preceding "final" major decisions (e.g., occupation, college major, etc.).

2.2 Testing for Willingness to Respond

The key to testing at this level of the *Affective Taxonomy* is the devising of appraisal situations in which willingness or consent can be noted directly or inferred from the behavior exhibited.

One approach to testing for *Willingness to respond* has already been described and illustrated at the previous level. This is to determine whether the behavior proceeds from choice or from an outside instigation by asking the student, in as subtle a manner as possible, about the reasons for his behavior. Of course, asking him to compose a response of his own assumes that he is conscious of the dynamics underlying the behavior and that he can verbalize them. Often he may be able to do neither.

Certain types of behaviors are in themselves direct evidence of *Willingness to respond.* Having hobbies, withdrawing of books from the library in addition to those required for assignments and book reports, corresponding with pen pals, becoming very knowledgeable about a subject—all are examples of behaviors in which there is a high voluntary component.

The student's display of interest in what he is doing is a definite sign of 2.2 behavior. Such positive reactions can be systematically noted in ongoing class behavior or by setting up paper-and-pencil test situations in which the student makes preferences among activities he has performed or indicates to what extent he wants to continue activities already begun at the teacher's request.

The display of co-operative behavior can also be considered as evidence of *Willingness to respond.* Those students actively taking part in selling magazine subscriptions to pay for a class trip are doing this willingly. But the conclusion should not be drawn that the students who do not ring door bells do not want to take part in this project. Some of them may not feel comfortable as salesmen, or they may be afraid of rebukes. Evidence of their *Willingness to respond* can be evinced from other behaviors, such as keeping records, depositing money in the bank, and making posters.

Movement from level 2.1 to level 2.2 can often be noted when the teacher no longer has to exert pressure on the student to perform. Exhibition of student behavior in the absence of suggestion and reminder can be noted by an observer if he develops a method for keeping a record of incidents of such behavior. Continuing activity beyond the minimum requirements is in itself a definite sign of *Willingness to respond.*

There is a variety of situations that can be set up in which *Willingness to respond* is inferred from student behavior. These are situations which occur in most classrooms as a normal part of the instructional effort. An example is the assignment of book reports and term papers. Assuming that the topics assigned are sufficiently attractive to elicit 2.2 behavior, a variety of behaviors which all students display in executing the assignment can singly, or preferably in combination, be used as cues to measure *Willingness to respond.* How early the student turns in the assignment is one cue. Using it is based on the assumption that the earlier the assignment is turned in, the greater is the likelihood that it was done willingly.

Other cues can also be used to appraise his affect. His doing much more research than was asked is one. The neatness of the report is another. The carefullness of the execution is a third. Reports that are neatly typed and carefully bound may reflect a greater *Willingness to respond* than those that contain fingerprint smudges and food stains.

Making an inference of *Willingness to respond* based on only one cue is fraught with error. Instead, we must look for a whole series of cues which, when woven together, possess an internal consistency and increase the probability that an interpretation of *Willingness to respond* is warranted.

At this level it is not necessary to ascertain the reasons for the *Willingness to respond.* Whether the student responds willingly in order to please the teacher[4] or because he is intrigued with the subject need not concern us.

2.2 Willingness to Respond—Selected Examples from the Test Literature

Illus. 2.2–A *Objective*: Willingness to be of service to the group of which he is a member.

Test: Adapted from *Self-Inventory of Personal-Social Relationships* (Chicago: Cooperative Study in General Education, American Council on Education, 1941).

Directions: 1. For each activity listed below mark your responses as follows in the column of A D letters at the left-hand side of the page:

Draw a circle around the A if the item represents an *activity in which you participate* or *something that you do,* either occasionally or frequently.

Draw a circle around the D if the item represents something you *rarely or never do.*

2. After you have responded to all items go back and reread all items for which you circled an A. For each one of these items mark a second response as follows in the column of W U letters at the right-hand side of the page:

Draw a circle around the W if you are interested in the item and you do it willingly.

Draw a circle around the U if you perform the activity with indifference or because someone feels that you should do it.

4.	A	D	Attending student-faculty teas.	W	U	(A,W)
13.	A	D	Organizing a social affair for a large group of students.	W	U	(A,W)
21.	A	D	Inviting college friends to visit my home.	W	U	(A,W)
37.	A	D	Being a leader in student government work —e.g., as a member of student council, chairman of committee, officer or a candidate for office, etc.	W	U	(A,W)

Illus. 2.2–B *Objective*: Assumes full responsibility for his duties as a member of a family.

Test: Adapted from *Interests and Activities; Test 8.2b* (Chicago: Evaluation in the Eight-Year Study, Progressive Education Association, 1939).

Directions: [Same as for Illustration 2.2–A, above.]

For girls:

8.	A	D	Helping get meals ready at home.	W	U	(A,W)
83.	A	D	Cleaning up after meals; drying or washing dishes.	W	U	(A,W)
108.	A	D	Helping someone in my family get ready to go out to a party.	W	U	(A,W)

For boys:

33.	A	D	Doing odd jobs around the house, such as fixing light sockets, mowing the lawn, etc.	W	U	(A,W)
58.	A	D	Helping to move or rearrange furniture.	W	U	(A,W)
63.	A	D	Helping mother carry the groceries home from the food store.	W	U	(A,W)

Illus. 2.2–C *Objective*: Engages in a variety of leisure-time reading activities.

Test: Adapted from *Questionnaire on Voluntary Reading; Test 3.32* (Chicago: Evaluation in the Eight-Year Study, Progressive Education Association, 1940).

Directions: There are three ways to mark the Answer Sheet:

Y means that your answer to the question is *Yes.*
U means that your answer to the question is *Uncertain.*
N means that your answer to the question is *No.*

11. Do you read the book-review sections of magazines or newspapers fairly regularly? (*Y*)
13. Do you often discuss with friends such questions as what the most popular current books are, what makes a book a best seller, and the like? (*Y*)
14. Is it rather unusual for you to read books, magazines, or newspapers for the particular purpose of learning more about authors and their works? (*N*)
36. Is it very unusual for you, of your own accord, to look up information about the life of an author after reading one of his books? (*N*)

---

[4]Of course, pleasing the teacher may be interpreted in many instances, as evidence of compliant or acquiescent behavior; that is, the student responds because it is expected of him. At the 2.2 *Willingness to respond* level, pleasing the teacher is a motive for learning that has intrinsic worth for the student. This is a subtle but important distinction, for the teacher's use of her influence or charisma as a positive factor is one of her major tools for working in the affective domain above the 2.1 level.

Comment on this illustration: Each of the items above is powerful enough to stand by itself as evidence of *Willingness to respond.* The more responses a student makes in the keyed direction, the greater is the likelihood that he is functioning at a higher level of the *Taxonomy.* In other words, these responses, when taken collectively, indicate a person who is no longer simply willing to respond. The student who reads book reviews regularly, discusses literary trends and events with friends, and investigates the lives of authors of books he reads is a person who is more than responding willingly. These activities are evidence of a deep commitment to things literary.

2.3 Satisfaction in Response

The additional element in the step beyond the *Willingness to respond,* the consent, the assent to responding, or the voluntary response is that the behavior is accompanied by a feeling of satisfaction, an emotional response, generally of pleasure, zest, or enjoyment.

Like the previous category, this is one in which we find a large number of objectives. The very specification that satisfaction accompanies the response designates a reinforcement or reward which tends to increase the frequency and strength of the response. The teacher who wishes to build a behavior which, once elicited, will have self-reinforcing qualities will find this category a useful one.[5]

[5] In some instances the educational objective is, implicitly or explicitly, to elicit *negative* emotional responses, such as revulsion, shock, distaste, not for their own sake but for some positive end. This is particularly true in social-studies instruction where learning is often facilitated, at least on the affective side, by playing upon these negative emotions. The educational objectives are stated positively, but the emotions elicited have negative valence. For example, developing an appreciation for democratic ideals by (among other things, of course) eliciting distaste for the racial policies of the Nazis. Or, eliciting shock when visiting urban slum areas in order to foster an appreciation of economic inequality. In this connection one is impressed with the potential educative power of highly dramatic and personally disturbing events like the upheaval in Little Rock over the admission of a few Negro children to all-white schools, the Detroit sit-down strikes of the 1930's, the atomic holocaust at Hiroshima, the Moscow purge trials, and the concentration camps of the Nazis.

A completely separate matter, of course, is that of negative learning experiences. These experiences produce affects which serve to repel the student from the object or phenomenon. Here we think, in particular, of cognitive experiences in the primary grades—in reading, in science, in arithmetic—which tend to extinguish existing interests, perhaps even enthusiasms, which the youngster developed at home during the preschool years. The recent ferment in constructing new types of instructional materials is traceable in part to an attempt to remedy this situation.

The locating of this category in the hierarchy has been a matter of great difficulty. Just where in the process of internalization the attachment of an emotional response, kick, or thrill to a behavior occurs has been hard to determine. For that matter there is some uncertainty as to whether the level of internalization at which it occurs may not depend on the particular behavior. We have even questioned whether it should be a category. If our structure is to be hierarchical, then each category should include the behavior in the next level below it. Satisfaction and emotionality of response are certainly a part of the upper subcategories of the category above this one, which is termed 3.0 *Valuing*. These valuing subcategories include such behaviors as pursuing, seeking, and wanting, which involve active manipulation to attain an affectively tinged goal. Yet the lowest level of valuing—that of *Acceptance of a value*—need not *necessarily* be accompanied by emotion. Having an opinion may mean that one has a belief that is held without emotional commitment or desire—one that is open to re-evaluation, since the evidence is not affirmed to be convincing.

It is equally clear, however, that the attachment of an emotional component to the response often occurs at the early responding stages, when there is not sufficient consistency or stability of response to designate the respondent as holding an opinion or a value. For that matter, *Willingness to respond* may be accompanied by a low level of emotionality, possibly of enthusiasm. Perhaps the real answer to this difficulty is that the emotional component appears gradually through the range of internalization categories and that it is more particularly relevant to certain behaviors and/or to behavior in certain areas, subject matter, or situations than to others. Thus the attempt to specify a given position in the hierarchy as *the* one at which the emotional component is added may be doomed to failure.

The category is arbitrarily placed at this point in the hierarchy where it seems to occur most frequently and where it is cited as or appears to be an important component of the objectives at this level on the continuum. The category's inclusion at this point serves the pragmatic purpose of reminding us of the presence of the emotional component and its value in the building of affective behaviors. But it should not be thought of as appearing and occurring at this one point in the continuum and thus destroying the hierarchy which we are attempting to build.

2.3 Satisfaction in Response—Illustrative Educational Objectives

Finds pleasure in reading for recreation.
Enjoys reading books on a variety of themes.
Derives satisfaction from singing with others.
Listens with pleasure to good music.
Responds emotionally to a work of art or musical composition.
Uses various art media for recreation or emotional release.
Enjoys an increasing variety of types of reading materials for recreation.
Enjoys constantly increasing variety of good dramatic and other programs on radio, television, and recordings.
Finds pleasure in listening to various kinds of vocal and instrumental music.
Discovers many new areas for reading as a pleasurable leisure-time activity—romance, humor, friendship, family relations, history and biography, etc.
Reads orally, especially poetry, for personal pleasure.
Takes pleasure in conversing with many different kinds of people.
Finds pleasure in joining with others in singing the great songs, old and new.
Enjoys listening to good music directly, on records, and on the radio and television.
Plays real number games for fun.
Develops a keen interest in his physical surroundings—in trees, flowers, birds, insects, stars, rocks, physical processes, and the like.
Personal satisfaction in carrying out sound health practices.
Enjoyment of literature, intellectually and aesthetically, as a means of personal enrichment and social understanding.
Enjoyment of participation in varied types of human relationships and in group undertakings.
Enjoyment of music and of works of art and craftsmanship as a means of personal enrichment.
Enjoyment of self-expression in music and in arts and crafts as another means of personal enrichment.

2.3 Testing for Satisfaction in Response

The essential testing task at this level is to determine whether a feeling of satisfaction or a positive emotional reaction accompanies a behavior. Did the student enjoy listening to the story? Did he enjoy reading the book he took out of the library? Does he get satisfaction in writing term papers? Did he get a thrill in witnessing a performance of *Turandot* at the opera house after it had been studied in his music course?

Emotional responses, even those that signify satisfaction and enjoyment, may not necessarily be overtly displayed. There may be an emotional reaction that is not revealed to others. Whether it is displayed overtly depends upon the individual and the situation. Some people carry their feelings and their emotional reactions on their sleeve; that is, almost everything they feel, they reveal. Others by nature are more guarded in displaying their emotions. They can enjoy an activity "silently." The enjoyment, however, is experienced. By the same token certain situations elicit overt emotional reactions, while others do not.

The testing for overt manifestations of satisfaction involves two matters: (1) deciding which behaviors are indicative of satisfaction; (2) developing a method of systematically recording the manifestations of satisfaction.

Examples of overt behaviors which can be taken as evidence of satisfaction are:

After a group has finished singing a number, one of them says, "That was great! Let's sing some more songs."

On a trip to a slum, overt comments of shame or disgust.

On a trip to the museum a student, upon viewing a certain painting, exclaims, "How lovely!"

At the end of a concert, students applaud at length and shout, "Bravo!" or "Encore!" with gusto.

Students laugh uproariously while watching a comedy being presented by the school drama club.

Students hum the melody as the orchestra plays it, or keep time with the music by moving their heads and shoulders or by tapping their feet.

Where the emotional reaction, if one has indeed been made, is not overtly displayed or cannot be observed because it is displayed in private (for example, while reading at home), we must devise a test situation in which we ask the student for his reactions to the experience. Here the essential task for the examiner is to get the student to recall and verbalize the reactions without distorting them. The examiner, again, must be on his guard not to force the student to respond in a socially approved direction. The student must feel free to say he disliked the opera and not have to worry about being punished for his response.

A wide range of appraisal methods can be used here. They vary in (1) degree of structure all the way from an objective technique, in which each alternative represents a different degree of satisfaction, to a free-response situation (in which an emotional reaction is an element in the construction), and (2) degree of directness, from a conscious and controlled response situation to a semiconscious projective one.

The objective situation can take the form of a check list, let us say, of novels. The task for the student is to indicate those he had read and then give each of these a rating in terms of whether or not he enjoyed reading it. Or the matching test model can be used. Here the task for the student is to choose from a longer list the three or four adjectives which he thinks describe his feelings when he read the book. Included in such a list of adjectives would be those that are descriptive of a wide variety of positive and negative emotional reactions. The set of adjectives the student selects would reveal the nature and extent of the satisfaction he derived from the reading.

Projective techniques can be very useful vehicles to elicit emotional responses. Here the test situation is devised in such a manner that the student reveals his feelings without being aware of what constitutes an acceptable response. The sentence-completion test is a good example of an instrument of this type.

Illus. 2.3–A Suppose the teacher of a course in the European novel wants to know how much satisfaction his students derived from the novels they read and also obtain some notion as to which novels gave the most satisfaction. Using the sentence-completion model, the examiner would construct a series of incomplete sentences similar to the following:

War and Peace gave me ______________________________.
If I were to write a book review of *Jean Christophe*, I would ______________________________.

The student is told to write in the blank space the very first thing that occurs to him. To elicit a rapid and spontaneous response and to minimize censorship, the examiner could read the incomplete statements or project them on a screen, one at a time, and allow a very short period for the response.

2.3 Satisfaction in Response—Selected Examples from the Test Literature

Illus. 2.3–B *Objective*: Finds pleasure in reading for recreation.

Test: Taken from *Satisfaction Found in Reading Fiction; Inventory H-B2* (Chicago: Cooperative Study in General Education, American Council on Education, 1942).

Directions: The following pages give you an opportunity to express some of your reactions to the reading of fiction. We all read fiction of some sort, novels or short stories, in books and magazines. From this reading we get various kinds of satisfactions depending chiefly on the kind of fiction read and on the mood we are in at the time. In one mood we may prefer one sort of story; under different circumstances we may prefer another. Or the same story may impress us differently at different times. In short, we react to *particular* pieces at *particular* times.

The statements which follow, however, ask for your *general* reactions. Naturally you cannot have an attitude toward fiction in general except by generalizing particular attitudes which you have had toward a number of different works at various times. Consequently, though you must think of particular instances, try to think of a large number of them and to generalize your attitude before you react to the following statements.

Read each statement carefully, then

(A) If you feel you *do* get this satisfaction from *your general reading of fiction*, blacken answer space A.

(U) If you are *uncertain* as to your general attitude, or if the statement seems *unclear* or *meaningless*, blacken answer space U.

(D) If you feel you *do not* get this satisfaction, blacken answer space D.

1. Finding rest and relaxation after a hard day's work. (A)
8. Being surprised by a clever ending. (A)
10. Trying to guess what various characters will do. (A)
11. Being stimulated emotionally. (A)
22. Being reminded of situations I myself have been in. (A)
23. Feeling the beauty of the author's style. (A)
25. Rereading a book I read and enjoyed as a child. (A)
27. Enjoying a good cry. (A)
80. Getting the enjoyment of following a good plot. (A)
117. Enjoying the suspense of waiting to see how the story is going to turn out. (A)
133. Learning about the problems of poverty and unemployment. (A)

Illus. 2.3–C *Objective*: Has satisfaction in reading the plays covered in a drama course.

Test: Adapted from *Inventory of Reader's Interest* (Chicago: Cooperative Study in General Education, American Council on Education, Form CCS 2552, mimeographed, no date).

Directions: [Eight blank lines, labelled A through H, appear on the cover page of the inventory. Students write in the names of eight plays which the examiner wants them to consider.]

Some reading experiences naturally provide more satisfaction than others, depending on the reader and on the conditions of the reading. Please report as accurately as you can the amount of satisfaction you received in reading the selections listed above by comparing them with one another in several ways according to directions which appear on the following pages. Make a special effort to report *your* reactions only; these will often not be the same as the reactions the author intended or those which other persons would have. Your answers will have nothing to do with "grades"; in fact, they cannot be graded.

2. There are some plays which one wishes to read more than once and others which one prefers not to read again. Please record your feeling concerning these plays by entering capital letters in the appropriate spaces at the right below:

(*a*) Probably will not wish to read again: ( ) ( ) ( ) ( ) ( ) ( ) ( ) ( )

(*b*) May wish sometime to read again: ( ) ( ) ( ) ( ) ( ) ( ) ( ) ( )

(*c*) Probably will wish to read again rather soon:[6] ( ) ( ) ( ) ( ) ( ) ( ) ( ) ( )

5. Though various satisfactions are obtained from the reading of plays, some plays seem to belong more definitely than others in the class of *entertainment*. Do any two or three of the plays seem to you to belong mainly in this class, as compared with the others?

Plays: ( ) ( ) ( )

6. Can you remember ever rereading words or sentences or larger parts of a play because of some kind of satisfaction or "thrill" which came again with the rereading?

Yes[6] No (Circle one)

7. If you were to reread any particular part of any one or two or three of these plays because of some satisfaction resulting, which part would it be?

Play Indicate the part briefly in your own words.[6]

( ) ____________________

( ) ____________________

( ) ____________________

Illus. 2.3–D *Objective*: Enjoys reading the books taken out of the school library voluntarily.

Test: Adapted from *Questionnaire on Voluntary Reading; Test 3.32* (Chicago: Evaluation in the Eight-Year Study, Progressive Education Association, 1940).

---

[6]These responses are keyed for 2.3 *Satisfaction in response*.

Directions: The purpose of this questionnaire is to discover how you really feel about the books you read in your leisure time. Consider each question carefully and answer it as *honestly* and as *frankly* as you possibly can. There are no "right" answers as such. It is not expected that your own feelings about books should be like those of anyone else. There are three ways to mark the Answer Sheet:

Y means that your answer to the question is *Yes.*
U means that your answer to the question is *Uncertain.*
N means that your answer to the question is *No.*

6. Do you often become so absorbed in your reading of a book that you are almost unaware of what is going on around you? (Y)
9. While you are reading, is it unusual for you to feel as if you are experiencing the emotions attributed to one of the characters? (N)
17. Is the satisfaction which you find in reading an interesting book ever as great as that which you find in seeing a good motion picture? (Y)
18. Do you ever spend time browsing in a library or bookstore? (Y)
35. While you are reading, is it unusual for you to feel as if you are participating in the events described by the author? (N)
44. Once you have begun a book, do you usually finish reading it within a few days' time? (Y)
59. Is it very unusual for you to become so enthusiastic about a book that you urge several of your friends to read it? (N)

Illus. 2.3–E *Objective*: Enjoys participating in humanistic activities.

Test: Taken from *Humanities Participation Form* (cited in Paul L. Dressel and Lewis B. Mayhew, *General Education: Explorations in Evaluation.* Washington: American Council on Education, 1954, pp. 143 ff.).

Sample item: You read short stories or novels

I
1. never (if you choose this answer do not mark anything for items II and III)
2. occasionally
3. frequently

II
1. with little or no enjoyment
2. with a fair amount of enjoyment[7]
3. with great pleasure[7]

III
1. just for the story
2. paying some attention to plot and characterization
3. making a detailed examination of the idea and structure of the work

[7] Responses keyed for 2.3 *Satisfaction in response.*

Illus. 2.3–F *Objective*: Finds pleasure in science activities.

Test: Adapted from *Interest Index; Test 8.2a* (Chicago: Evaluation in the Eight-Year Study, Progressive Education Association, 1939).

Directions: As you read each item below underline one of the four letters after the number of that item on the Answer Sheet.

Underline *S* if you feel you *do* get satisfaction from performing the activity.
Underline *U* if you are *uncertain* as to your reaction to performing the activity.
Underline *D* if you feel you *do not* get satisfaction from performing the activity.
Underline *X* if you have *never performed* the activity.

19. To experiment with plants to find out how various conditions of soil, water, and light affect their growth. (*S*)
24. To study rock formations and to learn how they developed. (*S*)
74. To visit an observatory to learn how astronomers study the stars. (*S*)
118. To read about how distances to inaccessible places are measured, such as from the earth to the sun, the height of a mountain, etc. (*S*)
171. To read about new scientific developments. (*S*)

3.0 VALUING

This is the only category headed by a term which is in common use in the expression of objectives by teachers. Further, it is employed in its usual sense: that a thing, phenomenon, or behavior has worth. This abstract concept of worth is in part a result of the individual's own valuing or assessment, but it is much more a social product that has been slowly internalized or accepted and has come to be used by the student as his own criterion of worth.

Behavior categorized at this level is sufficiently consistent and stable to have taken on the characteristics of a belief or an attitude. The learner displays this behavior with sufficient consistency in appropriate situations that he comes to be perceived as holding a value. At the lowest level of *Valuing,* he is at least willing to permit himself to be so perceived, and at the higher levels he may behave so as to further this impression actively.

The category gives more specificity to the term "value" than is present in its ordinary usage in that it defines three levels of *Valuing,* each representing a stage of deeper internalization. At the lowest level of *Valuing,* the student has what we might typically call a belief: he merely accepts a value, and so we call this level *Acceptance of a value.* At the highest level the term "commitment" or "conviction" is more appropriate than belief, with its connotation of "belief with little doubt."

That many objectives exist at this level is clear from the number of illustrations given, but the inculcation of values which is here denoted is just as obviously a matter of some dispute. The desirable outcomes of a socialization process which enables the individual to live with the ideals of our society will certainly be classified here. The teacher will attempt in many overt ways to model them for the student and to provide reinforcement for those students displaying them. But since the values of our society are not completely internally consistent (e.g. competition vs. co-operation), the task of the teacher is markedly complicated. At this level, however, we are not concerned with the relationships among values but rather with the internalization of a set of specified, ideal values.

To the extent that these inconsistencies exist, or that the ideal values taught diverge from the norm the learner has adopted (be it peer-group, parents, or community), the teacher will have great difficulty in achieving his goals at this deeply internalized level.

This is especially true in those instances where the student is heavily committed to values divergent from the cultural norm and where they are reinforced outside the school situation.

Viewed from another standpoint, the objectives classified here are the prime stuff from which the conscience of the individual is developed into active control of behavior.

This category will be found appropriate for many objectives that use the term "attitude" (as well as, of course, "value"). Often when we use the term "attitude" we imply that the individual is valuing, either positively or negatively, some behavior, phenomenon, or object. But the term "attitude" is also used to denote quite general sets toward phenomena as well as an orientation toward them. Again it is hoped that the classification of the behavior within the subcategories will lend a specificity of meaning that the term "attitude" lacks.

An important element of behavior characterized by *Valuing* is that it is motivated, not by the desire to comply or obey, but by the individual's commitment to the underlying value guiding the behavior. In the socialization process, the learner may conform externally to a number of socially desirable rules of behavior which he has only partially accepted as his own—has only partially internalized. The matter of determining the congruence between his internal state and the overt behavior is a measurement problem. As was noted in category 2.1 *Acquiescence in responding*, except for an occasional objective calling for compliant behavior, such behavior is not a part of educational objectives. Thus the divergence between internal commitment and external behavior is a problem for the evaluator and teacher to handle.

3.1 Acceptance of a Value

At this level we are concerned with the ascribing of worth to a phenomenon, behavior, object, etc. The term "belief," which is defined as "the emotional acceptance of a proposition or doctrine upon what one implicitly considers adequate ground" (English and English, 1958, p. 64), describes quite well what may be thought of as the dominant type of behavior classified. As will be noted in the succeeding subdivisions of this category, beliefs have varying degrees of certitude. At this lowest level of *Valuing* we are concerned with the lowest levels of certainty; that is, there is more of a readiness to re-evaluate one's position than at the higher levels. It is a position that is somewhat tentative; the belief is not yet firmly founded.

As mentioned in the preliminary discussion of *Valuing*, one of the distinguishing characteristics of this behavior is the consistency of response to the class of objects, phenomena, etc., with which the belief or attitude is identified. This is true even at this, the lowest level of *Valuing*, for it is implied that the value is internalized deeply enough to be a consistently controlling force on behavior.

In addition to consistency of response, behavior classified at the level of *Valuing* shows enough continuity with respect to appropriate objects, phenomena, etc., that the person is perceived by others as holding the belief or value. At the level we are describing here, he is both sufficiently consistent that others can identify the value and sufficiently committed that he is willing to be so identified.

3.1 Acceptance of a Value—Illustrative Educational Objectives

Continuing desire to develop the ability to speak and write effectively.

Desires to attain optimum health.

Grows in his sense of kinship with human beings of all nations.

Feels himself a member of groups which undertake to solve a common problem, whether local, national, or international.

Recognition of desire for democratic relations of husband and wife and of parents and children.

A sense of responsibility for listening to and participating in public discussion.

Acceptance of the place of worship in man's life.

Recognition of companionship as an essential element in the success of marriage.

Increased appetite and taste for what is good in literature.

3.1 Testing for Acceptance of a Value

In testing for *Acceptance of a value* we must go beyond mere satisfaction and pleasure in the response to those behaviors which can be taken as evidence of seeking or wanting an object because it has worth and is considered to be important in its own right.

Take reading as an example. There is certainly satisfaction in reading at 3.1. But it is more than just a thrill over an exciting story. The student now views reading as an important activity and exhibits certain behavior which is indicative of this. He browses in bookstores, or he reads book reviews, or he plans a summer reading program around a particular theme, or he reads biographical sketches of authors of works he has read, or, after completing a book, he reads what critics have said about it. Each of these behaviors indicates a positive sentiment toward reading and a belief that reading has intrinsic worth beyond just simple satisfaction. A student who exhibits any one of these behaviors is at the 3.1 level. But the display of a number of them is evidence of a higher level of *Valuing*.

Another type of indication of 3.1 behavior is seen when the reading takes on a deeper and richer quality. The student now identifies with the characters he admires. Or he seeks out friends who have also read the book to discuss the ideas in it that have stimulated him.

Acceptance of a value is also inferred when new interests emerge from reading. For example, the student becomes fascinated with problems of urban renewal and planning and seeks out the writings of those holding a variety of viewpoints on this matter. Reading, in this instance, is the springboard to new kinds of goal-directed activity.

Evidence of *Acceptance of a value* can therefore be collected by directly asking the student such questions as:

After you have read a book, do you usually find out something about the author and his reasons for writing the book?

When you go to the theater do you read the program's biographical notes on the actors?

After you have seen a stimulating movie, do you generally discuss its ideas with friends?

As a result of your reading did you become interested in such problems as crime, unemployment, and racial discrimination?

All these behaviors are evidences of "extra dividends" accruing from responding beyond pleasure and satisfaction.

The holding of particular beliefs and attitudes is also evidence of value acceptance. Believing that visiting a dentist every six months is essential to maintaining dental health is one example. Feeling that one should devote time to worth-while community activities is another. Stating that the school regulations concerning bicycle riding during school hours are important and essential is a third. These are expressions of sentiments. They indicate that the affect which has been attached to an object or phenomenon has become internalized.

The classic direct and structured test of attitudes and beliefs is the most common device for testing at this level. Such a test consists of a series of value-laden statements. The student considers each statement and indicates the extent to which he is in agreement with it. At this level of the *Affective Taxonomy* we are primarily interested in whether he accepts, rather than rejects, the value.

When the attitude scale possesses a high degree of internal consistency, relatively low positive scores can be taken as indicating a tentative holding of the value.

3.1 Acceptance of a Value—Selected Examples from the Test Literature

Illus. 3.1–A *Objective*: Appreciation of the place of reading in one's life.

Test: Taken from *Questionnaire on Voluntary Reading; Test 3.32* (Chicago: Evaluation in the Eight-Year Study, Progressive Education Association, 1940).

Directions: The purpose of this questionnaire is to discover what you really think about the reading which you do in your leisure time. Consider each question carefully and answer it as *honestly* and as *frankly* as you possibly can. There are no "right" answers as such. It is not expected that your own thoughts or feelings or activities relating to books should be like those of anyone else. There are three ways to mark the Answer Sheet:

Y means that your answer to the question is *Yes*.
U means that your answer to the question is *Uncertain*.
N means that your answer to the question is *No*.

8. Have you ever tried to become, in some respect, like a character whom you have read about and admired? (Y)
33. Are there any characters in books whom you feel you know almost as well as you know your own friends? (Y)
61. After you have read a book, are you usually interested in finding out what critics have said about it? (Y)

Illus. 3.1–B *Objective*: Desires to attain optimum health.

Test: *Health Attitudes; Inventory 1.4* (Chicago: Cooperative Study in General Education, American Council on Education, 1941).

Directions: The following statements in the test represent opinions about various phases of health. Since there are no right or wrong answers to the statements, you are to express your own point of view about them. Indicate how you really feel about each statement immediately after you read it. Do not pause too long on any one of them. Mark the Answer Sheet as follows:

If you *agree* with the whole statement, mark the space under the *A*.
If you are *uncertain* how you feel about the whole statement, mark the space under the *U*.
If you *disagree* with the whole statement, mark the space under the *D*.

5. One should adjust his diet until his weight conforms (within 3 to 4 pounds) to the figure given in height-age-weight tables. (*A*)
38. Failure to have a periodic physical examination is one characteristic of poor citizenship. (*A*)
50. Requiring a physical examination prior to marriage is not part of the natural way in which mating should take place. (*D*)
57. Legislation should be passed which would invoke a serious penalty on manufacturers of drugs who fail to caution on the dangers involved in the lay use of their products. (*A*)

Illus. 3.1–C *Objective*: Appreciates the role of economic factors in one's life.

Test: Taken from *Scale of Beliefs on Economic Issues, III* (Chicago: Evaluation in the Eight-Year Study, Progressive Education Association, dittoed, no date).

Problem No. 4: A very capable college student failed to make a passing grade in certain of his courses. He said that it was because he was forced to work so much to pay his expenses. According to the rules of the college, he should be dismissed from school. Working at jobs outside of school has not been considered adequate reason for failing to do satisfactory school work. However, many people fear that capable students without financial resources are being deprived of the opportunity of a college education. They believe that society should furnish the opportunity for people with ability to go to college. However, such a plan would mean that either the college or the government had to furnish money for many of the students. Many colleges simply cannot bear such an expense. On the other hand, if the government furnished aid, that would place a heavy burden on the public. What should be done about this situation?

Directions: Decide what you think about the courses of action and mark the appropriate spaces: A if you approve of the course of action; D if you disapprove; U if you are uncertain.

Courses of Action:

16. Students who cannot afford to go to college should be given some financial aid so they would not have to work so much. (A)

18. Practically nothing can be done to help students who don't have enough ability to carry their school work at the same time they are earning their way. (D)
19. Students who cannot afford a college education should be furnished adequate money to go to college without having to work at all. (A)
20. People who earn their living should not be required to do as much school work as other students. (D)

Scoring rationale: By itself each keyed response is no higher than *Acceptance of a value.* However, if there is a consistency in the responses over a series of items of this type, a *Commitment* to a value (3.3) would have to be inferred.

3.2 Preference for a Value

The provision for this subdivision arose out of a feeling that there were objectives that expressed a level of internalization between the mere acceptance of a value and commitment or conviction in the usual connotation of deep involvement in an area.

Behavior at this level implies not just the acceptance of a value to the point of being willing to be identified with it, but the individual is sufficiently committed to the value to pursue it, to seek it out, to want it.

3.2 Preference for a Value—Illustrative Educational Objectives

Assumes responsibility for drawing reticent members of a group into conversation.

Interest in enabling other persons to attain satisfaction of basic common needs.

Initiates group action for the improvement of health regulations.

Deliberately examines a variety of viewpoints on controversial issues with a view to forming opinions about them.

Influences governmental and service agencies, commercial organizations, and mass communication media by expressing opinions in letters to them.

Writes letters to the press on issues he feels strongly about.

Assumes an active role in current literary activities.

Actively participates in arranging for the showing of contemporary artistic efforts.

Preference for artistically appropriate choice, arrangement, and use of ordinary objects of the environment.

3.2 Testing for Preference for a Value

Preference for a value denotes an intermediate level of involvement between the *Acceptance of a value* and a full *Commitment* to it. The student's investment of his time and energy in the object or phenomenon is greater at this level than at the previous one, but less than at the 3.3 *Commitment* level.

Let us see how the increasing investment of time and energy can be inferred from reading behavior. At 3.1 *Acceptance of a value* a student indicates that his reading of books has produced an interest in such social problems as crime and poverty. In a word, as a result of much voluntary and satisfying general reading he accepts these matters as being important, or of value. This is the first step toward specialized reading. At the 3.2 *Preference for a value* level a greater investment of time and energy is reflected in his expressed preference for reading books on these problems over other types of reading matter. At the 3.3 *Commitment* level we find that this student has drawn up a plan for an extensive program of reading on these social problems.

At 3.2 *Preference for a value* there is an involvement of the student in the object or phenomenon. This involvement either takes the form of overt action (such as writing letters to the press, working for the improvement of health regulations, and aiding in the planning of a school art fair) or takes the form of an armchair inquiry which is characterized by a great deal of reflection on and speculation about the object or phenomenon.

Thus testing for *Preference for a value* essentially requires obtaining concrete evidence of (1) specialized interests or particular values within a given area of the curriculum, and (2) a preference for these interests or values over others, as reflected in particular modes of behavior or particular points of view.

The situational method is a most appropriate one for appraisal at the 3.2 *Preference for a value* level. The general formula for such an approach to testing is to devise a situation in which a wide variety of choices is available to the student. Consistency of choice is the criterion used to determine whether the student has a *Preference for a value*.

Illus. 3.2–A Take, for example, the objective "Preference for a nutritionally balanced diet." To test for this objective the appraisal situation could be set in the school cafeteria during a regular noon meal. The student is permitted to choose his meal freely from a wide range of foods. To limit the number of choices he can make, the student is told that the cost of the meal he chooses cannot exceed a certain amount. When he reaches the end of the serving line the nutritionist notes the student's choices on a check list. The pattern of choices is then analyzed by the examiner to determine its degree of nutritional balance.

Illus. 3.2–B To test for the 3.2 objective in art, "Seeks out examples of good art," the appraisal situation can be set in an art museum which the class visits. A semistructured record form is devised by the examiner, and a copy is given to each student. With it the student keeps a record of what he does, noting also how much time he spends on each activity. Analysis of his completed form indicates the extent to which his time and effort were spent in seeking out and looking at examples of good art. Where it is not practical to visit an art museum an alternate examining method would be to give the student a large number of reproductions of art which vary in quality from masterpieces to popular but mundane works. The task for the student would be to sort the reproductions into groups, each of which represents a different degree of preference. Evidence of *Preference for a value* can be inferred for those students whose "strong" preference groupings consist of works of art which are universally considered to be "good."

Illus. 3.2–C The written work of students, such as essays, book reports, and term papers, can be used to test for *Preference for a value.* For example, in reporting on a book he has read, the student, without being asked, considers those of its characteristics which make it good literature. Such a consideration is evidence of a level of *Preference* exemplified by 3.2. The student did not limit his report to just an explanation of why he enjoyed reading the book. On his own, he considered it at a deeper level and thereby exhibited his value.

3.2 Preference for a Value—Selected Examples from the Test Literature

Illus. 3.2–D *Objective*: Willingness to form judgments about books read.

Test: Taken from *Questionnaire on Voluntary Reading; Test 3.32* (Chicago: Evaluation in the Eight-Year Study, Progressive Education Association, 1940).

Directions: [The general directions have been given above in illustration *3.1–A*.]

There are three ways to mark the Answer Sheet:
Y means that your answer to the question is *Yes.*
U means that your answer to the question is *Uncertain.*
N means that your answer to the question is *No.*

62. Do you ever try to explain how, in your opinion, a book might have been improved? (Y)
63. Is it rather unusual for you to compare two or more books and come to a decision about the relative merits of each? (N)
89. Is it quite unusual for you to compare your opinion of a book with that of someone else? (N)

Illus. 3.2–E *Objective*: Preference for artistically appropriate choice.

Test: Taken from *Inventory of the Arts* (Chicago: Cooperative Study in General Education, American Council on Education). This inventory appears as Appendix H in Harold Baker Dunkel, *General Education in the Humanities* (Washington, D.C., American Council on Education, 1947), pp. 312–21.

Directions: In this inventory you are asked to express some of your reactions toward the arts.... Obviously we react differently to different fields of the arts, and to various works of art. The statements which follow, however, ask for your *general* reactions....

Read each statement carefully. Then indicate your reactions on the Answer Sheet by underlining one of the three letters after the number of the item. Underline:

A if you feel that this statement is a fairly adequate expression of your general opinion.
U if you are uncertain whether you agree or disagree with the opinion expressed in this statement.
D if you disagree with the opinion expressed in the statement.

134. A house should be constructed in accordance with the most advanced technological developments. It should be as rational in plan and structure as a modern factory is. (D)
138. The price of an art object is a valid indication of its artistic value. (D)
146. A still life does not convey any definite mood. (D)

Illus. 3.2–F *Objective*: Wants to develop insight about people through the reading of novels.

Test: Taken from *Satisfactions Found in Reading Fiction; Inventory H-B2* (Chicago: Cooperative Study in General Education, American Council on Education, 1942).

Directions: [The general directions have been given above in illustration *2.3–B*.]

Read each statement carefully. Then:

(A) If you feel you *do* get satisfaction from *your general reading of fiction*, blacken answer space A.

(U) If you are *uncertain* as to your general attitude, or if the statement seems *unclear* or *meaningless*, blacken answer space U.

(D) If you feel you *do not* get this satisfaction, blacken answer space D.

23. Gaining insights which enable me to understand why people act as they do. (A)
74. Learning how people come to hold attitudes and beliefs which seem strange or silly to me. (A)
78. Getting insight into the beauties and problems of love and marriage. (A)
112. Learning how some of my own peculiarities may appear to other people. (A)

3.3 Commitment

Belief at this level involves a high degree of certainty. The ideas of "conviction" and "certainty beyond a shadow of a doubt" help to convey further the level of behavior intended. In some instances this may border on faith, in the sense of it being a firm emotional acceptance of a belief upon admittedly nonrational grounds. Loyalty to a position, group, or cause would also be classified here.

The person who displays behavior at this level is clearly perceived as holding the value. He acts to further the thing valued in some way, to extend the possibility of his developing it, to deepen his involvement with it and with the things representing it. He tries to convince others and seeks converts to his cause.

In contrast to the lowest level of *Valuing* and its preceding levels, there is a tension here which needs to be satisfied. In 2.3 *Satisfaction in response* the learner derives pleasure, but this is not necessarily sought because of an urgent need for this pleasurable satisfaction. At 3.3 the action is the result of an aroused need or drive. There is a real motivation to act out the behavior.

3.3 Commitment—Illustrative Educational Objectives

Loyalty to the various groups in which one holds membership.
Acceptance of the role of religion in personal and family living.
Loyalty to the social goals of a free society and a world community.

Faith in the power of reason and in the methods of experiment and discussion.
Devotion to those ideas and ideals which are the foundation of democracy.

3.3 Testing for Commitment

The following characteristics are central to our notion of *Commitment.* Collecting evidence on them must therefore represent the main thrust of a program of testing for this level of the *Affective Taxonomy.*

1. The valuing of an object or phenomenon endures over a period of time. Commitment is never a momentary or occasional enthusiasm or passion which is here today and gone tomorrow or next week, to be replaced by another temporary passion. When testing for *Commitment* the examiner must collect evidence on (*a*) how long the value has been held, and (*b*) how likely it is that the value will continue to be held.

2. The holding of the value over an extended period of time is not in itself sufficient evidence of a commitment to it. There must also be a considerable investment of energy in the object or phenomenon that is valued. It is as though the object has taken hold of the student, and he, at the same time, has taken hold of the object. The student is so engrossed with it that he talks about it at many opportunities and relates it to a host of other matters. Testing for this aspect of *Commitment* requires collecting evidence of drive and perseverance or evidence that the pursuing of a highly valued object satisfies a deep need.

3. There should be actions in behalf of the value, belief, or sentiment—actions which by their very nature imply a commitment. For example, as a consequence of the social-studies objective "Identification with a current social problem," one student volunteers to assist a juvenile-delinquent group worker in a neighborhood community center and devotes every Saturday during the school year to this work, while another student becomes interested in capital punishment and reads widely on the subject, attends lectures and public meetings, and talks with public officials and criminologists. It is these types of actions which the evaluator looks for when testing for *Commitment.*

There are instances in which the student is committed to a view but has never had the opportunity to act in behalf of it. The examiner must then construct a testing situation which not only elicits the belief but also provides information on the student's willingness to act.

Illus. 3.3–A Consider, for example, the objective "Devotion to those ideas which are the foundation of democracy." One of these ideas, as applied directly to the school, deals with the grouping of students in a random fashion or according to ability, rather than according to such factors as social class or race. To test whether students are committed to this idea, the examiner could employ the technique of sociodrama to simulate a real situation, such as a wealthy mother protesting to the school principal over the assignment of her son to a class containing a preponderance of children from working-class homes. The student is assigned the role of the principal, and it is the way he deals with the mother and her complaint that serves as the basic data to determine whether a commitment to this idea is present. Evidence of *Commitment* would be inferred from a display of strong feeling and emotion coupled with some compelling arguments in behalf of the school's official position.

4. The student develops strong feelings about the object or phenomenon and is never reluctant to display them to others. If he is "taken" with the problem of capital punishment he will, when a Caryl Chessman or a Paul Crump case comes into the national limelight, freely communicate his views to others and will make every effort to convince them of the rightness of his position. Of course, his very commitment is revealed when he is well-versed intellectually with the many facets of the problem and when he can ably, as well as willingly, defend his point of view in the face of an attack upon it.

A variety of techniques, both of the disguised and direct types, is available for the measurement of attitudes, beliefs, and values and can be used as models for measuring values considered to be outcomes of educational objectives. High scores on these instruments can, at best, be taken as evidence of *Preference for a value.* They generally do not provide evidence on *Commitment* since they do not consider the essential matters of the amount of time and energy invested by the student in behalf of the value he holds. These matters are most conveniently appraised by means of detailed questionnaires and inventories.

3.3 Commitment—Selected Examples from the Test Literature

Illus. 3.3–B *Objective*: Active involvement in current social or political problems.

Test: Adapted from *Interest Index; Test 8.2a* (Chicago: Evaluation in the Eight-Year Study, Progressive Education Association, 1939).

Directions: For each of the following activities mark:

A if you perform the activity occasionally or frequently.
N if you never perform the activity.

13. Attend public meetings to protest against something which you regard as unfair. (*A*)
63. Write about political or social issues, problems, or events, such as bills passed by Congress, revolutions, etc. (*A*)
188. Study the history of present political and social problems to find out what causes them and what has been done about such problems in the past. (*A*)

Illus. 3.3–C *Objective*: Devotion to reading as an avenue for self-improvement.

Test: Taken from *Questionnaire on Voluntary Reading; Test 3.32* (Chicago: Evaluation in the Eight-Year Study, Progressive Education Association, 1940).

Directions: [The general directions have been given above in illustration *3.1–A*.]

Y means that your answer to the question is *Yes.*
U means that your answer to the question is *Uncertain.*
N means that your answer to the question is *No.*

25. Do you find that the reading of books is of little help to you in understanding yourself and your own problems more clearly? (*N*)
47. Have any of the books which you have read markedly influenced your choice of a life vocation? (*Y*)
72. Is it very unusual for you to gain from your reading of books a better understanding of some of the problems which people face in their everyday living? (N)

Illus. 3.3–D *Objective*: Devotion to those ideas and ideals which are the foundation of democracy.

Test: Taken from *Social Beliefs; Test 4.31* (Chicago: Evaluation in the Eight-Year Study, Progressive Education Association, 1944).

Directions: The statements in this test are expressions of opinions. They deal with unsettled questions, and *there are no right or wrong answers*. Please *express your point of view about them*. Indicate how you really feel about the issues expressed immediately after reading the statement. Do not pause too long on any one of them. Mark the Answer Sheet as follows:

A if you *agree* with the *whole statement*.
U if you are *uncertain* how you feel about the *whole statement*.
D if you *disagree* with the *whole statement*.

101. Freedom of speech should be denied all those groups and individuals that are working against democratic forms of government. (*D*)[1]
125. Negroes should not be allowed to fill positions involving leadership of white people. (*D*)
189. The masses of the people have too little intelligence to vote wisely on important social issues. (*D*)

Illus. 3.3–E *Objective*: Devotion to the improvement of relations between students of different racial and religious backgrounds.

Test: Taken from *Beliefs About School Life; Test 4.6* (Chicago: Evaluation in the Eight-Year Study, Progressive Education Association, 1940).

Directions: The statements in the test booklet represent opinions about various phases of school life. Since there are no right or wrong answers to the statements, you are to express your own point of view about them. Indicate how you really feel about each statement immediately after you read it. Do not pause too long on any one of them. Mark the Answer Sheet as follows:

A if you *agree* with the *whole statement*.
U if you are *uncertain* how you feel about the *whole statement*.
D if you *disagree* with the *whole statement*.

15. It is better for Negro and white pupils to eat at different lunchroom tables. (*D*)
26. Pupils of different races (white, Negro, Japanese, etc.) should not dance with each other at school dances. (*D*)
54. A capable Negro pupil would make just as good a president of the student council as a capable white pupil. (*A*)
60. Jewish pupils and pupils who are not Jewish should not have dates with each other. (*D*)

[1]The keying of these items is in terms of the objective as stated. However, other objectives may be stated so as to make *A* (agree) responses evidence of *Commitment*. Such objectives would not be desirable ones from certain American points of view.

4.0 ORGANIZATION

As the learner successively internalizes values, he encounters situations for which more than one value is relevant. Thus necessity arises for (*a*) the organization of the values into a system, (*b*) the determination of the interrelationships among them, and (*c*) the establishment of the dominant and pervasive ones. Such a system is built gradually, subject to change as new values are incorporated. In the adult, changes are made with much greater effort and difficulty than in the child; the organization becomes more rigid with age and less ready to accept a value inconsistent with those already embraced.

The category 4.0 *Organization* is intended as the proper classification for objectives which describe the beginnings of the building of a value system. It is subdivided into two levels, since a prerequisite to interrelating is the conceptualization of the value in a form which permits organization. Thus *Conceptualization* forms the first subdivision in the process, *Organization of a value system* forming the second.

While the order of the two subcategories seems appropriate enough with reference to one another, it is not so certain that 4.1 *Conceptualization of a value* is properly placed as the next level above 3.3 *Commitment.* Conceptualization undoubtedly begins at an earlier level for some objectives. Thus in many instances commitment to a value will be accompanied by conceptualization as the student goes out of his way to argue and verbally defend his point of view. Like 2.3 *Satisfaction in response*, it is doubtful that a single completely satisfactory location for this category can be found. Positioning it before 4.2 *Organization of a value system* appropriately indicates a prerequisite of such a system. It also calls attention to a component of affective growth that occurs at least by this point on the continuum but may begin earlier.

In this connection it should be noted that verbalization is not necessarily the same as conceptualization. Verbalization of enthusiasm, for instance, is a very low level of conceptualization. At the *Conceptualization* level we are particularly concerned with higher-level cognitive behavior such as *Analysis* and *Synthesis.* It is acknowledged that such a high level of cognitive behavior may not be necessary to holding an attitude so far as actual behavior is concerned. For that matter, Rhine notes, "People often betray by their behavior, attitudes which they do not recognize as their own" (Rhine, 1958, p. 363). But this is not true of school objectives, which are our concern in the *Taxonomy*. In school objectives there is an attempt to provide the child a conscious base for making choices. Thus he will be able to defend his choices if challenged and will know the basis of his attitudes regarding what is good. Such learning is also likely to be more permanent and less weakened by attack.

4.1 Conceptualization of a Value

In the previous category, 3.0 *Valuing*, we noted that consistency and stability are integral characteristics of the particular value or belief. At this level (4.1) the quality of abstraction or conceptualization is added. This permits the individual to see how the value relates to those that he already holds or to new ones that he is coming to hold.

Conceptualization may or may not be verbal. It will be abstract, and in this sense it will be symbolic. But the symbols need not be verbal symbols. An artist may express his feelings in terms of media with which he is familiar; the composer, in still different terms. As the viewer of abstract art is already aware, neither of these men may communicate to others, but the process may still clarify the interrelations of concepts for the artist—and this is the kind of behavior which is to be classified here. Whether conceptualization first appears at this point on the affective continuum is a moot point which was considered in the discussion of the nature of 4.0 *Organization*.

The process of abstraction, involving as it does the determination of commonalities, includes the processes of analysis and differentiation. The building of a concept requires both the process of abstraction and that of generalization. The process of abstraction isolates the properties which are the characteristics of the particular concept involved, and the generalization recognizes the application of the concept to a wider set of data than that from which it was originally derived. Thus the concept represents knowledge that is not directly perceived through the senses but rather results from manipulation of the sensory impressions in abstract form.

Many of the objectives which will be placed here may be worded in such a way that they appear to call for the comparative evaluation of values. Thus the objective "Begins to form judgments as to the responsibility of society for conserving human and material resources" appears to call for the comparative evaluation of various values to determine the responsibility of society. Indeed, it could probably mean just that in some situations; but it could also mean that the teacher wished the student to internalize a value which related to conservation of resources and wished him to be able to conceptualize it. Thus for proper classification of objectives here, perhaps more than in some of the other categories, some additional interpretation of their meaning by the classifier will be required. In looking over some of the other objectives placed in this category, the reader will find some in which only a portion of the objective belongs at this level (e.g., the example just given). As stated, these may possess the appearance of cognitive objectives which require the process of evaluation. But they are properly classified here when they imply the necessity of conceptualizing the value to provide a basis for their evaluation and interrelationship with other values.

4.1 Conceptualization of a Value—Illustrative Educational Objectives

Attempts to identify the characteristics of an art object which he admires.

Finding out and crystallizing the basic assumptions which underlie codes of ethics and are the basis of faith.

Forms judgments as to the responsibility of society for conserving human and material resources.

Relates his own ethical standards and personal goals through the reading of biography and other appropriate literature.

4.1 Testing for Conceptualization of a Value

In all previous sections on evaluating affective outcomes of instruction, measurement has always been in terms of discrete objectives and phenomena. We have discussed various strategies for evaluating the stages in the ongoing process of internalizing a particular object. When we move to the 4.1 level, we are dealing with the *Conceptualization of a value* of an object, action, or attitude so that this value can be integrated into the student's value system. The process of conceptualization is largely cognitive, involving abstraction and generalization.

The testing program seeks for evidence that higher-order cognitive abilities have actually been called into play. The emphasis is less on the quality of the cognitive processes than on the fact that they are being used. We do not want to test directly for the ability to evaluate. Rather, we want to know whether comparative evaluation of values actually has taken place after it has been demonstrated that a particular value has emerged.

There are, basically, three major types of evidence that we seek at this level. Each type can be taken as indicating value conceptualization: (1) evidence that the student has developed evaluative judgments with regard to the object he values; (2) evidence of abstract or symbolic thinking about the valued object; (3) evidence of generalization about a set or class of values of which the valued object is a member.

Such evidence appears when the student is very much taken with the object and now considers it in a deeper sense. For example, he desires to evaluate those musical works and composers that he appreciates and values highly. He compares one composer with another or looks for evidence of change and growth in the life work of a particular composer. Or he seeks to analyze an art masterpiece to determine its universal characteristics.

At the previous level (3.3 *Commitment*), we mentioned the student who has a commitment to the problem of capital punishment. In a sense, his commitment is at a concrete level, characterized by a desire to communicate his feelings and convictions and do something toward solving the problem. At the level of value conceptualization (4.1) the problem is perceived more broadly. This new view has now taken on an abstract quality. The famous capital punishment cases are related to each other in an attempt to discover and understand common characteristics. The basic assumptions underlying capital punishment are examined, as well as theories of crime and consideration of the central role that society plays in this problem.[1]

---

[1]These are, strictly speaking, cognitive behaviors. They are interpreted here as evidence of value conceptualization (4.1) because they could not have been undertaken without a great deal of affect having developed.

4.1 Conceptualization of a Value—Selected Examples from the Test Literature

Illus. 4.1–A *Objective*: Develops a rationale as to the place of the citizen in a democracy.

Test: Taken from *Social Beliefs; Test 4.31* (Chicago: Evaluation in the Eight-Year Study, Progressive Education Association, 1944).

Directions: The statements in this test are expressions of opinion. They deal with unsettled questions, and there are no right or wrong answers. Please express your point of view about them. Mark the Answer Sheet as follows:

A if you *agree* with the *whole statement.*
U if you are *uncertain* how you feel about the *whole statement.*
D if you *disagree* with the *whole statement.*

102. In deciding whether a law is constitutional, the Supreme Court should consider the contributions of the law to the welfare of the people as more important than its strict agreement with the Constitution. (*A*)
115. Every citizen should support measures that provide for public health facilities, relief, and other urgent community needs, even though these would increase his taxes. (*A*)
136. The personal and political beliefs of a worker should not be permitted to affect his chances for employment and promotion. (*A*)

Illus. 4.1–B *Objective*: Uses reading to derive ideas about the conduct of life.

Test: Adapted from *Satisfaction Found in Reading Fiction; Inventory H-B2* (Chicago: Cooperative Study in General Education, American Council on Education, 1942).

Directions: [The general directions have been given above in illustration *2.3–B.*]

Read each statement carefully. Then mark:
A if the statement *does apply* to your reading.
U if you are *uncertain* as to whether the statement applies to you in your reading.
D if the statement *does not apply* to your reading.

44. Realizing that I do not stand alone in certain of the ideas and beliefs I hold. (*A*)
92. Being encouraged by finding that other people are apparently troubled by the same sorts of problems and difficulties I am. (*A*)
124. Being able to see many different patterns of life portrayed and the author's idea of what happens to people who adopt this kind of life. (*A*)
128. Finding ideas which I can make part of my own philosophy of life. (*A*)

4.2 Organization of a Value System

Objectives properly classified here are those which require the learner to bring together a complex of values, possibly disparate values, and to bring these into an ordered relationship with one another. Ideally, the ordered relationship will be one which is harmonious and internally consistent. This is, of course, the goal of such objectives, which seek to have the student formulate a philosophy of life. In actuality, the integration may be something less than entirely harmonious. More likely the relationship is better described as a kind of dynamic equilibrium which is, in part, dependent upon those portions of the environment which are salient at any point in time.

The placing of concepts into an order or into the right locus in a context of concepts is not the only type of behavior properly classified here. In many instances the organization of values may result in their synthesis into a new value or value complex of a higher order. For example, the objective that "work and play should be balanced" is a distinction which is not meaningful when we change the objective to read that "the individual should choose work that will be sufficiently enjoyable to him that it yields the same rewards as recreation." In this instance, work and play are combined into a single behavior, and the original distinction no longer obtains.

4.2 Organization of a Value System—Illustrative Educational Objectives

Weighs alternative social policies and practices against the standards of the public welfare rather than the advantage of specialized and narrow interest groups.

Attempts to determine how conception of a democratic society can be related to the conservation of human and material resources.

Forms judgments as to how the respect for human dignity can be related to the directions in which American society will move in the next decade.

Realistic acceptance of an emotional adjustment to the limitations inherent in his own aptitudes, abilities, interests, and physical conditions.

Judges people of various races, cultures, national origins, and occupations in terms of their behaviors as individuals.

Develops techniques for controlling aggression in culturally acceptable patterns.

Develops a plan for regulating his rest in accordance with the demands of his activities.

Begins to form judgments as to the major directions in which American society should move.

4.2 Testing for Organization of a Value System

The testing for a value system essentially involves (1) the identification of the component parts of the student's value system (that is, the values, beliefs, and sentiments which he has "taken into" his value system) and (2) the identification of the pattern of values in the system. This pattern indicates the interrelationships among the values; that is, those that are dominant or central in the student's life and those that occupy a more peripheral position in his system.

The latter requirement can take as its general model the large number of inventories and schedules which attempt to measure aspects of personality. Among the better-known instruments of this type are the *Minnesota Multiphasic Personality Inventory*, Cattell's *Sixteen Personality Factor Questionnaire*, the Edwards' *Personal Preference Schedule*, and Allport, Vernon, and Lindzey's *Study of Values*.

These tests are "trait-oriented" in the sense that they measure a set of personality traits, or a set of needs, or a set of values, each set having its origin either in personality theory or in previous empirical studies which employ multivariate analytic techniques to produce such a set. The important fact to note here is that the set of traits is usually represented as a more or less self-contained system.

Illus. 4.2–A Generally, a group of test items is assembled into a scale to measure each trait in the set, and a score is then derived for each trait. Interpretation is based on the pattern of an individual's scores. Rather than consider each score as a separate entity, the set of traits is looked at as a system of interrelated traits, and the individual is characterized by the pattern of score relationships obtained for him.[2] Each pattern can be described as having a unique ordering of its parts. If the traits in the set are indeed measuring different parts of a system rather than all measuring the same general phenomenon, as is often the case, we can then determine which of the traits are the dominant and pervasive ones and which are minor or peripheral.

In using this type of instrument as the model for testing for *Organization of a value system*, the examiner's starting point is

---

[2]It is not within the scope of this discussion to consider the vital matter of the validity of the profiles obtained.

the valuing-level of the educational objective to be evaluated. He can measure the strength of this value in a context of values which are not in harmony with it, or he can measure it against values which are known to have been internalized and conceptualized previously.

Illus. 4.2–B There are other ways of collecting evidence on the pervasiveness of a particular value. Take, for example, the objective "Rejects stereotypes of people of various races, cultures, national origins, and occupations." Here we want to devise evaluation situations which allow the student either to reject stereotypes presented to him or to give his views on, or perception of, particular social groups. An example of a situation which tests for the former approach is to present the student with a series of pictures, each of which shows a member of a social or occupational group in a stereotyped role or making a stereotypical statement. The task for the student is to indicate what he finds pleasurable or objectionable, if anything, in each picture. Evidence of 4.2 is inferred where there is a consistency in rejecting the false generalizations of the stereotypes.

Illus. 4.2-C It may be preferable at times to arrange for an evaluation situation which produces such stereotyped values spontaneously. The technique of psychodrama could be very useful in the evaluation of this educational objective. The student, for example, is instructed to play the role of a personnel manager of a plant interviewing a Negro applicant for the position of foreman of a group of white machinists who have pronounced anti-Negro sentiments. The role of the applicant is played by a fellow student according to rather precise guidelines. Evaluation of the personnel manager role is in terms of the degree to which the student exhibited stereotypical behavior toward the applicant.

4.2 Organization of a Value System—Selected Examples from the Test Literature

Illus. 4.2-D *Objective*: Begins to form judgments concerning the type of life he wants to lead.

Test: Asahel D. Woodruff, *A Study of Choices*. In Asahel Davis Woodruff, *A Study of the Directive Factors in Individual Behavior* (Ph.D. thesis, University of Chicago, June, 1941).

Description of the Test: This test yields a profile which consists of the following twelve values: Money, Society, Political, Social Service, Home Life, Comfort, Religion, Security, Personal Attractiveness, Excitement, Friends, Intellectual Activity.

Scores are obtained on each of these twelve values by exposing the student to three basic problems which, he is told, "he is likely to face in the very near future." The three problems are: (1) selection of a place (town) to live, (2) selection of a social group to join, and (3) selection of a vocation.

Let us look at the first problem to see how the values are derived. Detailed descriptions of eight different places are presented. Here are the descriptions of place No. 1 and place No. 8, representing the extreme points in the array of places:

Place No. 1: This place offers rather unusual opportunities both in your line of work and for additional income in other ways, and the *chances of making money fast are good.* Some have even *made fortunes here.* There is very little society life, and scanty chance for political activity, as a powerful clique is well entrenched and does not permit interference. There is a fair school system, and the townspeople are, on the whole, progressive and successful. Most people are admittedly here for the business opportunities, and many plan to move elsewhere when they have enough to retire on. Keeping up with the competition requires vigorous attention to work, and allows little for the armchair, or afternoons on the beach, or golf, etc.

Place No. 8: This place has pioneered in a program of *social and economic security for its citizens.* It has established a safe, practical method of *guaranteeing job or income security to all people* who, for any reasons, need such assistance. In other respects the place is no different from most others. You can earn a comfortable living here, you will have little or no political activity, your home life will be pleasant but often interrupted by outside duties. Social life and the inducements to recreation and relaxation are scarce.

The student goes through four steps in the consideration of each problem: "(1) A preliminary survey of the problem and the recording of a tentative selection of the two best and two worst solutions to the problem. (2) Expression of favorable and unfavorable comments for each available course of action in the problem. (3) A paired comparison analysis of the possible choices of action in the problem. (4) A final choice of the two best and the two worst courses of action."

The techniques for scoring and analysis of responses are rather detailed. Since it is not unusual to have to develop complex scoring procedures at this level of the *Affective Taxonomy*, Woodruff's summary of these procedures from pages 154–55 of his thesis should give the reader a sense of what may be involved at this level:

The value pattern shown in each problem is combined with those shown in the other two problems and a composite pattern is depicted on the score sheet. Comments recorded in the answer booklet are summarized and the frequency of positive and negative mention of each value is shown opposite the value pattern.

The following five test scores are developed from analysis of the relation of the person's reactions in each problem to his reactions in the other problems, and for the inter-relationship of his reactions in the four parts of each problem.

1. The *rho score* shows the amount of consistency in the rank position each value occupies in its two appearances in the total test. The score is derived by means of Spearman's rank correlation formula, using as the two sets of variables the ranked lists of values as of their first and second appearance in the total test. This score is believed to show, with some reservations, the degree of constancy of the rank order of values for an individual in all three problems.

2. The *A score* shows the extent to which the individual was able to make choices in the initial survey of each problem which were not changed in any subsequent analysis of the same problem. This score is believed to show something resembling insight into the problem and its meaning for the person's values.

3. The *B score* shows the relative ability of an individual to recognize instances in which his analysis of a problem tends to alter his earlier major choices in the problem. This score is believed to show the individual's awareness of the implications for values of detailed actions and choices, and his ability to relate such choices to his major decisions, and vice versa.

4. The *C score* shows the relative extent to which individuals contradict their initial decisions by their detailed choices in subsequent analyses of the problems, and fail to recognize such contradictions, or at least fail to show such recognition by making the final choices agree with the preferences in the detailed analyses. This score is believed to be an index of failure to comprehend the effects of detailed acts on major goals.

5. The *D score* shows the amount of inconsistent choosing in the paired comparisons of each problem, and is believed to be an index of uncertainty or confusion concerning the relative worth of any two or more values.

Illus. 4.2–E *Objective*: Begins to develop dominant values.

Test: G. W. Allport, P. E. Vernon, and Gardner Lindzey, *Study of Values*, Third edition (Boston: Houghton Mifflin Company, 1960).

Directions: Each of the following situations or questions is followed by four possible attitudes or answers. Arrange these answers in the order of your personal preference by writing, in the appropriate box at the right, a score of 4, 3, 2, or 1. To the statement you prefer most give 4, to the statement that is second most attractive 3, and so on.

2. In your opinion, can a man who works in business all the week best spend Sunday in
   a. trying to educate himself by reading serious books.
   b. trying to win at golf, or racing.
   c. going to an orchestral concert.
   d. hearing a really good sermon.

15. Viewing Leonardo da Vinci's picture, "The Last Supper," would you tend to think of it
    a. as expressing the highest spiritual aspirations and emotions.
    b. as one of the most priceless and irreplaceable pictures ever painted.
    c. in relation to Leonardo's versatility and its place in history.
    d. the quintessence of harmony and design.

Comment: The profile obtained for this test is the basic datum for evaluation at 4.2. This profile consists of six fundamental values based directly upon the typology of Eduard Spranger. These six types of values are: (1) Theoretical, (2) Economic, (3) Aesthetic, (4) Social, (5) Political, (6) Religious.

5.0 CHARACTERIZATION BY A VALUE OR VALUE COMPLEX

At this level of internalization the values already have a place in the individual's value hierarchy, are organized into some kind of internally consistent system, have controlled the behavior of the individual for a sufficient time that he has adapted to behaving this way; and an evocation of the behavior no longer arouses emotion or affect except when the individual is threatened or challenged.

Here the individual is described in terms of (*a*) his unique personal characteristics—that is, the basic threads or sets of orientations which account for a great range of disparate behavior—and (*b*) his philosophy of life or world view—the principles and ideals, the personal credo, which provide an integration and a consistency for the various aspects of his life.

Thus the individual acts consistently in accordance with the values he has internalized at this level, and our concern is to indicate two things: (*a*) the generalization of this control to so much of the individual's behavior that he is described and characterized as a person by these pervasive controlling tendencies and (*b*) the integration of these beliefs, ideas, and attitudes into a total philosophy or world view. These two aspects constitute the subcategories.

Rarely, if ever, are the sights of educational objectives set to this level of the *Affective Taxonomy*. Realistically, formal education generally cannot reach this level, at least in our society. In all open and pluralistic societies, such as our own, the maturity and personal integration required at this level are not attained until at least some years after the individual has completed his formal education. Time and experience must interact with affective and cognitive learnings before the individual can answer the crucial questions, "Who am I?" and "What do I stand for?"

In the more traditional society a philosophy of life, a mode of conduct, is spelled out for its members at an early stage in their lives. A major function of education in such a society is to achieve the internalization of this philosophy.

This is not to suggest that education in an open society does not attempt to develop personal and social values. It does indeed.

But more than in traditional societies it allows the individual a great amount of freedom in which to achieve a *Weltanschauung.*[1]

At this, the highest level of the *Affective Taxonomy,* the relation between cognitive and affective processes becomes very pronounced. We can say that the man who has achieved a philosophy of life—a man who knows who he is—has arrived at this truth through painful intellectual effort in which the more complex mental processes of the *Cognitive Taxonomy* are clearly functioning.

5.1 Generalized Set

The generalized set is that which gives an internal consistency to the system of attitudes and values at any particular moment. It is selective responding at a very high level. It is sometimes spoken of as a determining tendency, an orientation toward phenomena, or a predisposition to act in a certain way. But unlike the track star poised for the starter's gun, the generalized set is a response to highly generalized phenomena. It is a persistent and consistent response to a family of related situations or objects. Further, in contrast to the track star's conscious concentrated attention to the crack of the gun, it may often be an unconscious set which guides action without conscious forethought.

The generalized set may be thought of as closely related to the idea of an attitude cluster, where the commonality is based on behavioral characteristics rather than the subject or object of the attitude. Thus an attitude cluster involving attitudes toward persons of different races would not be of concern to us here, but an attitude cluster which had as a common thread a willingness to accept factual evidence would be thought of as a generalized set. It is the behavioral component with which we are concerned.

A generalized set should not be equated with behaving narrowly or blindly. We prefer to think of it as a basic orientation which enables the individual to reduce and order the complex world about him and to act consistently and effectively in it. This basic orientation relates a whole series of attitudes, values, and

---

[1]Often this is too challenging a goal for the individual to achieve on his own, and the net effect is either maladjustment or the embracing of a philosophy of life developed by others. Cf. Erich Fromm, 1941; T. W. Adorno *et al.*, 1950.

beliefs. To the outsider it is the thread which makes the individual predictable and comprehensible.

This is an important category of objectives. These generalized sets are important determiners of the way an individual approaches a problem, determining what he will see as important in it, delimiting the things which he will take into account in attempting to find a solution, and determining the tenacity with which he clings to the initial perception of the problem (thus determining the extent to which he will be unable to retreat from a blind alley). The behaviors included in it, though not properly a part of the cognitive domain, have a marked influence on the manner in which the behaviors learned in the cognitive domain will be employed in solving problems. If the student is not able to achieve certain of the objectives which would be properly categorized here at the same time that he achieves cognitive objectives, his ability to accomplish the cognitive behaviors will be imperfect, academic, and ultimately, in life, of much less value than they would otherwise be.

One may naturally ask whether the objectives classified here belong properly in the cognitive domain. These behaviors have been practiced so long that they are virtually devoid of affect in general usage; as already noted, some indeed are practiced unconsciously. But affect readily reappears in instances of threat or challenge. Further, they are the result, the culmination, of long practice with affective behavior. They derive from the way in which the individual handles the more affect-laden situations which are the concern of the categories at the levels below this one. They are slow to develop and represent the peak of assimilation by the individual of these patterns of action. As such they are not objectives which any single teacher, course, or even school can hope to achieve fully, or perhaps do more than approach with uncertain progress in the course of a semester or a year.

5.1 Generalized Set—Illustrative Educational Objectives

Readiness to revise judgments and to change behavior in the light of evidence.

Changes his mind when new facts or insights demonstrate the need for revision of opinions formerly held.

Willingness to face facts and conclusions that can be logically drawn from them.

Views problems in objective, realistic, and tolerant terms.

The habit of approaching problems objectively.

Acceptance of objectivity and systematic planning as basic methods in arriving at satisfying choices.

Relies increasingly upon the method of science in finding answers to questions about the physical world and about society.

Changes his opinion on controversial issues when an examination of the evidence and the arguments calls for revision of opinions previously held.

Confidence in his ability to succeed.

Judges problems in terms of situations, issues, purposes, and consequences involved rather than in terms of fixed, dogmatic precepts or emotionally wishful thinking.

5.1 Testing for Generalized Set

At this level the examiner is interested in collecting evidence about the student's basic orientations or points of view. These are the poses which characterize and give him a behavioral consistency; for example, approaching problems objectively, systematic planning, examination of evidence before making a decision, consideration of the consequences of his acts before acting, confidence in his ability to solve a problem, etc.

Illus. 5.1–A A major testing model at this level is rather straightforward, taking its form from the many studies of the effect of information upon social attitudes. We can present the model more clearly by showing how it can be employed to evaluate the 5.1 objective "Changes his opinion on controversial issues when an examination of the evidence and the arguments calls for revision of opinions previously held." The examiner first employs an attitude scale to determine the student's opinion on a controversial issue such as capital punishment. Then the cognitive core of the attitude is appraised by having the student state the major reasons for his holding such an opinion. When the opinion appears to have a weak cognitive base—that is, is based almost exclusively on hearsay or on emotion—the examiner presents the student with facts and information that are contrary to his view. Serious consideration of this information by the student, leading to a change in sentiment or a realization that the issue is more complex than he thought, suggests a 5.1 mode of approach. Specific attitudes and beliefs are stable phenomena. Also, controversial issues are, by definition, complex and multifaceted. Consequently there is little probability of a complete reversal of opinion in a short period of time and solely on the basis of the information obtained by the student in the test situation. Therefore the examiner must seek evidence not only that the student has not automatically rejected the information, but that some movement has occurred toward a change in view or toward taking a deeper view of the problem.

The great range of problem-solving tasks developed in research on human learning and thinking represents another fruitful source for the construction of 5.1 instruments. The major ingredient required in such instruments is that the problem be sufficiently subtle and complex for the student being tested that the generalized set which we wish to observe can be brought into play. We are not interested in whether the problem is solved accurately or with elegance. Nor are we interested in the cognitive steps that lead to the solution. Rather, at 5.1 we are concerned with the mode of approach: whether the student tackled the problem with care, with objectivity, and with confidence.

The various methods of rating and judging aspects of personality which have already been developed represent another major way of appraising 5.1 *Generalized Set.* At this level the essential task for the rater is to make judgments concerning those behavioral consistencies of the student which the school deems to be desirable. Of course the rater must possess a great deal of information about the student, preferably through extensive observation in structured situations. The rating scale, or scales, provides the means by which the rater can analyze and reduce the information he has collected.[2]

Projective techniques, particularly the picture interpretation type (e.g., the *Thematic Apperception Test*), seem to be potentially valuable for the measurement of 5.1 *Generalized Set.* Naturally, in an educational appraisal situation the examiner is not looking for abnormal or clinical material. Rather, he is seeking evidence of consistency among the student's stories with respect to that orientation or set which is the objective of the instructional effort. If the basic orientation to be developed is "Observation of details," then the stories must be analyzed in terms of this characteristic.

---

[2]An excellent treatment of rating techniques is Chapter VII of Vernon, 1953.

5.1 Generalized Set—Selected Illustrations from the Test Literature

Illus. 5.1–B *Objective*: Respect for the worth and dignity of human beings.

Test: Problems in Human Relations Test. Cited in Paul L. Dressel and Lewis B. Mayhew, *General Education: Explorations in Evaluation* (Washington: American Council on Education, 1954), pp. 229–37.

1. Tom and Bob who know each other only slightly were double-dating two girls who were roommates. A sudden storm made it impossible to go to the beach as planned. Tom suggested going to a movie. After making the suggestion, he realized Bob was without funds. As Tom, what would you do?
   (1) Pay for the party.
   (2) Lend Bob money.
   (3) Leave it up to the girls.
   *(4) Get Bob to suggest something.
   (5) Apologize to Bob for making the suggestion.
2. Your social organization has pledged a student who is not liked by some of the members. One of your friends threatens to leave the social organization if this person is initiated. What would you do?
   (1) Talk to your friend.
   (2) Do not initiate the prospective member.
   (3) Get more members to support the prospective member.
   *(4) Vote on the prospective member.
   (5) Postpone the vote until the matter works itself out.

Scoring rationale: The response marked with an asterisk is keyed to a point of view which the authors of the instrument call "Democratic."

5.2 CHARACTERIZATION

This, the peak of the internalization process, includes those objectives which are broadest with respect both to the phenomena covered and to the range of behavior which they comprise. Thus, here are found those objectives which concern one's view of the universe, one's philosophy of life, one's *Weltanschauung*—a value system having as its object the whole of what is known or knowable.

Objectives categorized here are more than generalized sets in the sense that they involve a greater inclusiveness and, within the group of attitudes, behaviors, beliefs, or ideas, an emphasis on internal consistency. Though this internal consistency may not always be exhibited behaviorally by the students toward whom the objective is directed, since we are categorizing teachers' objectives, this consistency feature will always be a component of *Characterization* objectives.

As the title of the category implies, these objectives are so encompassing that they tend to characterize the individual almost completely. One may properly question whether such a category as this should be included in a taxonomy intended to help teachers and research workers understand the meaning of their objectives and find ways to measure them.

5.2 Characterization—Illustrative Educational Objectives

Develops for regulation of one's personal and civic life a code of behavior based on ethical principles consistent with democratic ideals.

Develops a consistent philosophy of life.

Develops a conscience.

5.2 Testing for Characterization

The philosophy of life which emerges at this level can be viewed as a transfer of objectives and behaviors of the lower categories in the most general sense possible. The specific values and sentiments previously attached to particular objects have now become general phenomena, such as character and morality. For example, the commitment to social problems is transformed into a code of behavior which represents the central guiding principles in the individual's conduct of his life. In all his relations with other people he is characterized by kindness, respect, and humility. A consistency in behavior is clearly discernible among all the social roles he is required to assume and between the public and private domains of his life.

The great humanitarian figures of history—Socrates, Christ, Lincoln, Ghandi, Einstein—have achieved the characterization we refer to at this level. Each is universally held in high esteem precisely because his philosophy of life characterizes and pervades all of his behavior.

A major long-range outcome of education is the development of a consistent philosophy of life by the student. A basic tenet of liberal education is that it is by means of intellectual effort—learning, reflection, inquiry—that a philosophy of life in large measure is formed. However, it is the attainment of a philosophy of life, of a code for governing all of one's conduct, that is the ultimate goal of education. We want the student to lead the good life and become a good man in all his parts. In the words of the Harvard report on general education:

> Education must look to the whole man. It has been wisely said that education aims at the good man, the good citizen, and the useful man. By a good man is meant one who possesses an inner integration, poise, and firmness, which in the long run come from an adequate philosophy of life. Personal integration is not a fifth characteristic in addition to the other four and coordinate with them; it is their proper fruition.[3]

John W. Gardner, in considering the aims of a free people, speaks of the kind of person that is needed:

> The plain fact is that never in our history have we stood in such desperate need of men and women of intelligence, imagination and courage. The challenge is there—greater than any generation has ever faced. . . . But how should we rise to the challenge? What is important . . . is this: if you believe in a free society, be worthy of a free society. Every good man strengthens society . . . Men of integrity, by their very existence, rekindle the belief that as a people we can live above the level of moral squalor. We need that belief; a cynical community is a corrupt community.[4]

In a very real sense we are talking at this level about the attainment of maturity by the individual. Much has been written about maturity, but very little of it is useful to the examiner as a basis for testing. However, two developmental theories, one by Peck and Havighurst (1960) and the other by Erikson (1950), do offer valuable guidelines for instrument construction.

Peck and Havighurst, in an extensive study of character development among adolescents, postulated five character types, "each conceived as the representative of a successive stage in the psychosocial development of the individual":

Character Type	*Developmental Period*
Amoral	Infancy
Expedient	Early Childhood
Conforming	Later Childhood
Irrational-Conscientious	
Rational-Altruistic	Adolescence and Adulthood

---

[3] Harvard University Committee, 1945, p. 74.
[4] Gardner, 1961, pp. 153–54.

The last-named type strongly suggests our 5.2 level. This type is described as

having the tendency to act with consideration of others and their ultimate welfare. This is carried out both in terms of the possible effects over a time-span and on any other people who might be concerned, and in terms of a rationally held body of principles as to what constitutes the greatest good for the greatest number. These principles . . . have been modified and differentiated by conscious, rational assessment of their human significance.[5]

To identify people of this type Peck and Havighurst employed a large variety of clinical instruments and procedures, chief among which were: (1) intensive interviews; (2) projective techniques such as a sentence completion test, the *Rorschach Test*, the *Thematic Apperception Test*, essays on "The Person I Would Like to Be Like," "A Good Kind of Person in Our Community Is," "When I'm Twenty-Two"; (3) sociometric techniques consisting essentially of "guess who" tests involving character, social, and personality traits.

Erikson (1950, pp. 219–34) postulates that the adult has to pass successively through eight stages in order to achieve maturity. These eight stages represent a developmental hierarchy in which advancement depends upon a successful resolution of the basic or "nuclear" conflict which is representative of each stage. When the individual fails to cope successfully with the conflict, his development is arrested and he fixates at that stage. Erikson's eight stages and their basic conflicts are:

Development Period	*Basic Conflict*
Oral Sensory	Trust vs. Mistrust
Muscular-Anal	Autonomy vs. Shame
Locomotor-Genital	Initiative vs. Guilt
Latency	Industry vs. Inferiority
Puberty and Adolescence	Identity vs. Role Diffusion
Young Adulthood	Intimacy vs. Isolation
Adulthood	Generativity vs. Stagnation
Maturity	Integrity vs. Disgust, Despair

Erikson describes the achievement of integrity, which is the hallmark of maturity, as

the ego's accrued assurance of its proclivity for order and meaning. It is a post-narcissistic love of the human ego—not of the self—as an experience which conveys some world order and spiritual sense, no matter how dearly paid for. It

[5]Peck and Havighurst, 1960, pp. 3, 234.

is the acceptance of one's one and only life cycle as something that had to be and that, by necessity, permitted of no substitutions: it thus means a new, a different love of one's parents. . . . Although aware of the relativity of all the various life styles which have given meaning to human striving, the possessor of integrity is ready to defend the dignity of his own life style against all physical and economic threats. For he knows that an individual life is the accidental coincidence of but one life cycle with but one segment of history; and that for him all human integrity stands or falls with the one style of integrity of which he partakes. The style of integrity developed by his culture or civilization thus becomes the "patrimony of his soul," the seal of his moral paternity of himself. Before this final solution, death loses its sting.[6]

5.2 Characterization—Selected Examples from the Test Literature

Illus.
5.2–A

Test: General Goals of Life; Inventory H-A1b (Cooperative Study in General Education, American Council on Education, 1942).[7]

This inventory identifies the dominant life goals of the college student. Twenty life goals are employed, each reflected in a representative statement. The student is presented with 190 pairs of statements (each life goal statement is paired once with all the other nineteen) and is asked to indicate which statement of the pair "is a more nearly adequate expression of your main life goal."

Example of statements of life goals are:

A. Serving God, doing God's will.
B. Achieving personal immortality in heaven.
C. Self-discipline—overcoming my irrational emotions and sensuous desires.
E. Doing my duty.
G. Serving the community of which I am a part.
J. Finding my place in life and accepting it.
N. Making a place for myself in the world; getting ahead.
P. Security—protecting my way of life against adverse changes.
S. Survival, continued existence.
T. Handling the specific problems of life as they arise.

The score for any goal is the number of times it was chosen in preference to other goals. Thus the maximum score for a dominant goal is 19.

Students are at 5.2 if (1) the array of their scores reveals both high-score and low-score clusters and (2) the elements of the high-score cluster "hang together" meaningfully. Thus, in the two score patterns shown below, Student A is functioning at level 5.2, whereas Student B is only at level 3.3 because high and

[6] Erikson, 1950, p. 232.

[7] For a detailed description of the rationale and uses of this test see Dunkel, 1947, pp. 21–78.

low scoring clusters do not exist:

STUDENT A		STUDENT B	
Score	*Life Goal*	*Score*	*Life Goal*
19	Serving God	14	Power, control of others
18	Achieving personal immortality	14	Getting ahead
17	Doing my duty	14	Living for the pleasure of the moment
16	Self-discipline	12	Doing my duty
15	Self-sacrifice	11	Survival, continued existence
* *			
4	Getting as many pleasures out of life as I can	7	Peace of mind, contentment
3	Handling the specific problems of life as they arise	5	Finding my place in life
2	Getting ahead	5	Serving God
1	Living for the pleasure of the moment		
0	Survival, continued existence		

Illus. 5.2–B

Test: *Inventory of Beliefs*; Form T. Cited in G. C. Stern, M. I. Stein, and B. S. Bloom, *Methods in Personality Assessment* (Glencoe, Ill.: The Free Press, 1956), pp. 187–215.

This inventory was constructed to yield evidence on Stern, Stein, and Bloom's model for the characterization of personality. The model consists of three syndromes, each varying in its basic psychological characteristics along eight designated "major personality parameters." For example, the characteristics of each syndrome on dimension 1, "Reaction to Others," and dimension 5, "Energy Level," are:

(S) STEREOPATH SYNDROME	(H) NON-STEREOPATH SYNDROME	(R) RATIONAL SYNDROME
	Reactions to Others	
Depersonalization of relationships. Perception of authority figures as omnipotent, threatening, and impregnable.	Highly personalized relationships. Perception of authority figures realistically, frequently as overprotective or overpossessive.	Little emotional involvement in personal relationships. Perception of authority figures as distant, vulnerable and fallible.
	Energy Level	
Ineffectual liberation of affective tension and continual free-floating anxiety drains off energy otherwise available for goal-directed activity.	Capable of sustained effort for remote goals.	Moderate to strong, directed chiefly toward abstract pursuits, sometimes impractical in content.

APPENDIX A

A Condensed Version
of the Affective Domain of the
Taxonomy of Educational Objectives

1.0 RECEIVING (ATTENDING)

At this level we are concerned that the learner be sensitized to the existence of certain phenomena and stimuli; that is, that he be willing to receive or to attend to them. This is clearly the first and crucial step if the learner is to be properly oriented to learn what the teacher intends that he will. To indicate that this is the bottom rung of the ladder, however, is not at all to imply that the teacher is starting *de novo.* Because of previous experience (formal or informal), the student brings to each situation a point of view or set which may facilitate or hinder his recognition of the phenomena to which the teacher is trying to sensitize him.

The category of *Receiving* has been divided into three subcategories to indicate three different levels of attending to phenomena. While the division points between the subcategories are arbitrary, the subcategories do represent a continuum. From an extremely passive position or role on the part of the learner, where the sole responsibility for the evocation of the behavior rests with the teacher—that is, the responsibility rests with him for "capturing" the student's attention—the continuum extends to a point at which the learner directs his attention, at least at a semiconscious level, toward the preferred stimuli.

1.1 AWARENESS

Awareness is almost a cognitive behavior. But unlike *Knowledge,* the lowest level of the cognitive domain, we are not so much concerned with a memory of, or ability to recall, an item or fact as we are that, given appropriate opportunity, the learner will merely be conscious of something—that he take into account a situation, phenomenon, object, or stage of affairs. Like *Knowledge* it does not imply an assessment of the qualities or nature of the stimulus, but unlike *Knowledge* it does not necessarily imply attention. There can be simple awareness without specific discrimination or recognition of the objective characteristics of the object, even though these characteristics must be deemed to have an effect. The individual may not be able to verbalize the aspects of the stimulus which cause the awareness.

Develops awareness of aesthetic factors in dress, furnishings, architecture, city design, good art, and the like.

Develops some consciousness of color, form, arrangement, and design in the objects and structures around him and in descriptive or symbolic representations of people, things, and situations.[1]

1.2 WILLINGNESS TO RECEIVE

In this category we have come a step up the ladder but are still dealing with what appears to be cognitive behavior. At a minimum level, we are here describing the behavior of being willing to tolerate a given stimulus, not to avoid it. Like *Awareness,* it involves a neutrality or suspended judgment toward the stimulus. At this level of the continuum the teacher is not concerned that the student seek it out, nor even, perhaps, that in an environment crowded with many other stimuli the learner will necessarily attend to the stimulus. Rather, at worst, given the opportunity to attend in a field with relatively few competing stimuli, the learner is not actively seeking to avoid it. At best, he is willing to take notice of the phenomenon and give it his attention.

Attends (carefully) when others speak—in direct conversation, on the telephone, in audiences.

Appreciation (tolerance) of cultural patterns exhibited by individuals from other groups—religious, social, political, economic, national, etc.

Increase in sensitivity to human need and pressing social problems.

1.3 CONTROLLED OR SELECTED ATTENTION

At a somewhat higher level we are concerned with a new phenomenon, the differentiation of a given stimulus into figure

---

[1] Illustrative objectives selected from the literature follow the description of each subcategory.

and ground at a conscious or perhaps semiconscious level—the differentiation of aspects of a stimulus which is perceived as clearly marked off from adjacent impressions. The perception is still without tension or assessment, and the student may not know the technical terms or symbols with which to describe it correctly or precisely to others. In some instances it may refer not so much to the selectivity of attention as to the control of attention, so that when certain stimuli are present they will be attended to. There is an element of the learner's controlling the attention here, so that the favored stimulus is selected and attended to despite competing and distracting stimuli.

Listens to music with some discrimination as to its mood and meaning and with some recognition of the contributions of various musical elements and instruments to the total effect.

Alertness toward human values and judgments on life as they are recorded in literature.

2.0 RESPONDING

At this level we are concerned with responses which go beyond merely attending to the phenomenon. The student is sufficiently motivated that he is not just 1.2 *Willing to attend,* but perhaps it is correct to say that he is actively attending. As a first stage in a "learning by doing" process the student is committing himself in some small measure to the phenomena involved. This is a very low level of commitment, and we would not say at this level that this was "a value of his" or that he had "such and such an attitude." These terms belong to the next higher level that we describe. But we could say that he is doing something with or about the phenomenon besides merely perceiving it, as would be true at the next level below this of 1.3 *Controlled or selected attention.*

This is the category that many teachers will find best describes their "interest" objectives. Most commonly we use the term to indicate the desire that a child become sufficiently involved in or committed to a subject, phenomenon, or activity that he will seek it out and gain satisfaction from working with it or engaging in it.

2.1 ACQUIESCENCE IN RESPONDING

We might use the word "obedience" or "compliance" to describe this behavior. As both of these terms indicate, there is a passiveness so far as the initiation of the behavior is concerned, and the stimulus calling for this behavior is not subtle. Compliance is perhaps a better term than obedience, since there is more of the element of reaction to a suggestion and less of the implication of resistance or yielding unwillingly. The student makes the response, but he has not fully accepted the necessity for doing so.

Willingness to comply with health regulations.
Obeys the playground regulations.

2.2 WILLINGNESS TO RESPOND

The key to this level is in the term "willingness," with its implication of capacity for voluntary activity. There is the implication that the learner is sufficiently committed to exhibiting the behavior that he does so not just because of a fear of punishment, but "on his own" or voluntarily. It may help to note that the element of resistance or of yielding unwillingly, which is possibly present at the previous level, is here replaced with consent or proceeding from one's own choice.

Acquaints himself with significant current issues in international, political, social, and economic affairs through voluntary reading and discussion.

Acceptance of responsibility for his own health and for the protection of the health of others.

2.3 SATISFACTION IN RESPONSE

The additional element in the step beyond the *Willingness to respond* level, the consent, the assent to responding, or the voluntary response, is that the behavior is accompanied by a feeling of satisfaction, an emotional response, generally of pleasure, zest, or enjoyment. The location of this category in the hierarchy has given us a great deal of difficulty. Just where in the process of internalization the attachment of an emotional response, kick, or thrill to a behavior occurs has been hard to determine. For that matter there is some uncertainty as to whether the level of internalization at which it occurs may not depend on the particular behavior. We have even questioned whether it should be a category. If our structure is to be a hierarchy, then each category should include the behavior in the next level below it. The emotional component appears gradually through the range of internalization categories. The attempt to specify a given position in the hierarchy as *the* one at which the emotional component is added is doomed to failure.

The category is arbitrarily placed at this point in the hierarchy where it seems to appear most frequently and where it is cited as or appears to be an important component of the objectives at this level on the continuum. The category's inclusion at this point serves the pragmatic purpose of reminding us of the presence of the emotional component and its value in the building of affective behaviors. But it should not be thought of as appearing and occurring at this one point in the continuum and thus destroying the hierarchy which we are attempting to build.

Enjoyment of self-expression in music and in arts and crafts as another means of personal enrichment.

Finds pleasure in reading for recreation.

Takes pleasure in conversing with many different kinds of people.

3.0 VALUING

This is the only category headed by a term which is in common use in the expression of objectives by teachers. Further, it is employed in its usual sense: that a thing, phenomenon, or behavior has worth. This abstract concept of worth is in part a result of the individual's own valuing or assessment, but it is much more a social product that has been slowly internalized or accepted and has come to be used by the student as his own criterion of worth.

Behavior categorized at this level is sufficiently consistent and stable to have taken on the characteristics of a belief or an attitude. The learner displays this behavior with sufficient consistency in appropriate situations that he comes to be perceived as holding a value. At this level, we are not concerned with the relationships among values but rather with the internalization of a set of specified, ideal, values. Viewed from another standpoint, the objectives classified here are the prime stuff from which the conscience of the individual is developed into active control of behavior.

This category will be found appropriate for many objectives that use the term "attitude" (as well as, of course, "value").

An important element of behavior characterized by *Valuing* is that it is motivated, not by the desire to comply or obey, but by the individual's commitment to the underlying value guiding the behavior.

3.1 ACCEPTANCE OF A VALUE

At this level we are concerned with the ascribing of worth to a phenomenon, behavior, object, etc. The term "belief," which is defined as "the emotional acceptance of a proposition or doctrine upon what one implicitly considers adequate ground" (English and English, 1958, p. 64), describes quite well what may be thought of as the dominant characteristic here. Beliefs have varying degrees of certitude. At this lowest level of *Valuing* we are concerned with the lowest levels of certainty; that is, there is more of a readiness to re-evaluate one's position than at the higher levels. It is a position that is somewhat tentative.

One of the distinguishing characteristics of this behavior is consistency of response to the class of objects, phenomena, etc. with which the belief or attitude is identified. It is consistent enough so that the person is perceived by others as holding the belief or value. At the level we are describing here, he is both sufficiently consistent that others can identify the value, and sufficiently committed that he is willing to be so identified.

Continuing desire to develop the ability to speak and write effectively.
Grows in his sense of kinship with human beings of all nations.

3.2 PREFERENCE FOR A VALUE

The provision for this subdivision arose out of a feeling that there were objectives that expressed a level of internalization between the mere acceptance of a value and commitment or conviction in the usual connotation of deep involvement in an area. Behavior at this level implies not just the acceptance of a value to the point of being willing to be identified with it, but the individual is sufficiently committed to the value to pursue it, to seek it out, to want it.

Assumes responsibility for drawing reticent members of a group into conversation.

Deliberately examines a variety of viewpoints on controversial issues with a view to forming opinions about them.

Actively participates in arranging for the showing of contemporary artistic efforts.

3.3 COMMITMENT

Belief at this level involves a high degree of certainty. The ideas of "conviction" and "certainty beyond a shadow of a doubt" help to convey further the level of behavior intended. In some instances this may border on faith, in the sense of it being a firm emotional acceptance of a belief upon admittedly nonrational grounds. Loyalty to a position, group, or cause would also be classified here.

The person who displays behavior at this level is clearly perceived as holding the value. He acts to further the thing valued in some way, to extend the possibility of his developing it, to deepen his involvement with it and with the things representing it. He tries to convince others and seeks converts to his cause. There is a tension here which needs to be satisfied; action is the result of an aroused need or drive. There is a real motivation to act out the behavior.

Devotion to those ideas and ideals which are the foundations of democracy.

Faith in the power of reason and in methods of experiment and discussion.

4.0 ORGANIZATION

As the learner successively internalizes values, he encounters situations for which more than one value is relevant. Thus necessity arises for (*a*) the organization of the values into a system, (*b*) the determination of the interrelationships among them, and (*c*) the establishment of the dominant and pervasive ones. Such a system is built gradually, subject to change as new values are incorporated. This category is intended as the proper classification for objectives which describe the beginnings of the building of a value system. It is subdivided into two levels, since a prerequisite to interrelating is the conceptualization of the value in a form which permits organization. *Conceptualization* forms the first subdivision in the organization process, *Organization of a value system* the second.

While the order of the two subcategories seems appropriate enough with reference to one another, it is not so certain that 4.1 *Conceptualization of a value* is properly placed as the next level above 3.3 *Commitment*. Conceptualization undoubtedly begins at an earlier level for some objectives. Like 2.3 *Satisfaction in response*, it is doubtful that a single completely satisfactory location for this category can be found. Positioning it before 4.2 *Organization of a value system* appropriately indicates a prerequisite of such a system. It also calls attention to a component of affective growth that occurs at least by this point on the continuum but may begin earlier.

4.1 CONCEPTUALIZATION OF A VALUE

In the previous category, 3.0 *Valuing*, we noted that consistency and stability are integral characteristics of the particular value or belief. At this level (4.1) the quality of abstraction or conceptualization is added. This permits the individual to see how the value relates to those that he already holds or to new ones that he is coming to hold.

Conceptualization will be abstract, and in this sense it will be symbolic. But the symbols need not be verbal symbols. Whether conceptualization first appears at this point on the affective continuum is a moot point, as noted above.

Attempts to identify the characteristics of an art object which he admires.

Forms judgments as to the responsibility of society for conserving human and material resources.

4.2 ORGANIZATION OF A VALUE SYSTEM

Objectives properly classified here are those which require the learner to bring together a complex of values, possibly disparate values, and to bring these into an ordered relationship with one another. Ideally, the ordered relationship will be one which is harmonious and internally consistent. This is, of course, the goal of such objectives, which seek to have the student formulate a philosophy of life. In actuality, the integration may be something less than entirely harmonious. More likely the relationship is better described as a kind of dynamic equilibrium which is, in part, dependent upon those portions of the environment which are salient at any point in time. In many instances the organization of values may result in their synthesis into a new value or value complex of a higher order.

Weighs alternative social policies and practices against the standards of the public welfare rather than the advantage of specialized and narrow interest groups.

Develops a plan for regulating his rest in accordance with the demands of his activities.

5.0 CHARACTERIZATION BY A VALUE OR VALUE COMPLEX

At this level of internalization the values already have a place in the individual's value hierarchy, are organized into some kind of internally consistent system, have controlled the behavior of the individual for a sufficient time that he has adapted to behaving this way; and an evocation of the behavior no longer arouses emotion or affect except when the individual is threatened or challenged.

The individual acts consistently in accordance with the values he has internalized at this level, and our concern is to indicate two things: (*a*) the generalization of this control to so much of the individual's behavior that he is described and characterized as a person by these pervasive controlling tendencies, and (*b*) the integration of these beliefs, ideas, and attitudes into a total philosophy or world view. These two aspects constitute the subcategories.

5.1 GENERALIZED SET

The generalized set is that which gives an internal consistency to the system of attitudes and values at any particular moment. It is selective responding at a very high level. It is sometimes spoken of as a determining tendency, an orientation toward phenomena, or a predisposition to act in a certain way. The generalized set is a response to highly generalized phenomena. It is a persistent and consistent response to a family of related situations or objects. It may often be an unconscious set which guides action without conscious forethought. The generalized set may be thought of as closely related to the idea of an attitude cluster, where the commonality is based on behavioral characteristics rather than the subject or object of the attitude. A generalized set is a basic orientation which enables the individual to reduce and order the complex world about him and to act consistently and effectively in it.

Readiness to revise judgments and to change behavior in the light of evidence.

Judges problems and issues in terms of situations, issues, purposes, and consequences involved rather than in terms of fixed, dogmatic precepts or emotionally wishful thinking.

5.2 CHARACTERIZATION

This, the peak of the internalization process, includes those objectives which are broadest with respect both to the phenomena covered and to the range of behavior which they comprise. Thus, here are found those objectives which concern one's view of the universe, one's philosophy of life, one's *Weltanschauung*—a value system having as its object the whole of what is known or knowable.

Objectives categorized here are more than generalized sets in the sense that they involve a greater inclusiveness and, within the group of attitudes, behaviors, beliefs, or ideas, an emphasis on internal consistency. Though this internal consistency may not always be exhibited behaviorally by the students toward whom the objective is directed, since we are categorizing teachers' objectives, this consistency feature will always be a component of *Characterization* objectives.

As the title of the category implies, these objectives are so encompassing that they tend to characterize the individual almost completely.

Develops for regulation of one's personal and civic life a code of behavior based on ethical principles consistent with democratic ideals.

Develops a consistent philosophy of life.

APPENDIX B

A Condensed Version
of the Cognitive Domain of the
Taxonomy of Educational Objectives

KNOWLEDGE

1.00 KNOWLEDGE

Knowledge, as defined here, involves the recall of specifics and universals, the recall of methods and processes, or the recall of a pattern, structure, or setting. For measurement purposes, the recall situation involves little more than bringing to mind the appropriate material. Although some alteration of the material may be required, this is a relatively minor part of the task. The knowledge objectives emphasize most the psychological processes of remembering. The process of relating is also involved in that a knowledge test situation requires the organization and reorganization of a problem such that it will furnish the appropriate signals and cues for the information and knowledge the individual possesses. To use an analogy, if one thinks of the mind as a file, the problem in a knowledge test situation is that of finding in the problem or task the appropriate signals, cues, and clues which will most effectively bring out whatever knowledge is filed or stored.

1.10 KNOWLEDGE OF SPECIFICS

The recall of specific and isolable bits of information. The emphasis is on symbols with concrete referents. This material, which is at a very low level of abstraction, may be thought of as the elements from which more complex and abstract forms of knowledge are built.

1.11 Knowledge of Terminology

Knowledge of the referents for specific symbols (verbal and nonverbal). This may include knowledge of the most generally accepted symbol referent, knowledge of the variety of symbols which may be used for a single referent, or knowledge of the referent most appropriate to a given use of a symbol.

To define technical terms by giving their attributes, properties, or relations.

Familiarity with a large number of words in their common range of meanings.[1]

1.12 Knowledge of Specific Facts

Knowledge of dates, events, persons, places, etc. This may include very precise and specific information such as the specific date or exact magnitude of a phenomenon. It may also include approximate or relative information such as an approximate time period or the general order of magnitude of a phenomenon.

The recall of major facts about particular cultures.

The possession of a minimum knowledge about the organisms studied in the laboratory.

1.20 Knowledge of Ways and Means of Dealing with Specifics

Knowledge of the ways of organizing, studying, judging, and criticizing. This includes the methods of inquiry, the chronological sequences, and the standards of judgment within a field as well as the patterns of organization through which the areas of the fields themselves are determined and internally organized. This knowledge is at an intermediate level of abstraction between specific knowledge on the one hand and knowledge of universals on the other. It does not so much demand the activity of the student in using the materials as it does a more passive awareness of their nature.

1.21 Knowledge of Conventions

Knowledge of characteristic ways of treating and presenting ideas and phenomena. For purposes of communication and consistency, workers in a field employ usages, styles, practices, and forms which best suit their purposes and/or which appear to suit best the phenomena with which they deal. It should be

[1]Each subcategory is followed by illustrative educational objectives selected from the literature.

recognized that although these forms and conventions are likely to be set up on arbitrary, accidental, or authoritative bases, they are retained because of the general agreement or concurrence of individuals concerned with the subject, phenomena, or problem.

Familiarity with the forms and conventions of the major types of works; e.g., verse, plays, scientific papers, etc.

To make pupils conscious of correct form and usage in speech and writing.

1.22 Knowledge of Trends and Sequences

Knowledge of the processes, directions, and movements of phenomena with respect to time.

Understanding of the continuity and development of American culture as exemplified in American life.

Knowledge of the basic trends underlying the development of public assistance programs.

1.23 Knowledge of Classifications and Categories

Knowledge of the classes, sets, divisions, and arrangements which are regarded as fundamental for a given subject field, purpose, argument, or problem.

To recognize the area encompassed by various kinds of problems or materials.

Becoming familiar with a range of types of literature.

1.24 Knowledge of Criteria

Knowledge of the criteria by which facts, principles, opinions, and conduct are tested or judged.

Familiarity with criteria for judgment appropriate to the type of work and the purpose for which it is read.

Knowledge of criteria for the evaluation of recreational activities.

1.25 Knowledge of Methodology

Knowledge of the methods of inquiry, techniques, and procedures employed in a particular subject field as well as those employed in investigating particular problems and phenomena. The emphasis here is on the individual's knowledge of the method rather than his ability to use the method.

Knowledge of scientific methods for evaluating health concepts.

The student shall know the methods of attack relevant to the kinds of problems of concern to the social sciences.

1.30 Knowledge of the Universals and Abstractions in a Field

Knowledge of the major schemes and patterns by which phenomena and ideas are organized. These are the large structures, theories, and generalizations which dominate a subject field or which are quite generally used in studying phenomena or solving problems. These are at the highest levels of abstraction and complexity.

1.31 Knowledge of Principles and Generalizations

Knowledge of particular abstractions which summarize observations of phenomena. These are the abstractions which are of value in explaining, describing, predicting, or in determining the most appropriate and relevant action or direction to be taken.

Knowledge of the important principles by which our experience with biological phenomena is summarized.

The recall of major generalizations about particular cultures.

1.32 Knowledge of Theories and Structures

Knowledge of the *body* of principles and generalizations together with their interrelations which present a clear, rounded, and systematic view of a complex phenomenon, problem, or field. These are the most abstract formulations, and they can be used to show the interrelation and organization of a great range of specifics.

The recall of major theories about particular cultures.

Knowledge of a relatively complete formulation of the theory of evolution.

INTELLECTUAL ABILITIES AND SKILLS

Abilities and skills refer to organized modes of operation and generalized techniques for dealing with materials and problems. The materials and problems may be of such a nature that little or no specialized and technical information is required. Such information as is required can be assumed to be part of the individual's general fund of knowledge. Other problems may require specialized and technical information at a rather high level such that specific knowledge and skill in dealing with the problem and the materials are required. The abilities and skills objectives emphasize the mental processes of organizing and reorganizing material to achieve a particular purpose. The materials may be given or remembered.

2.00 COMPREHENSION

This represents the lowest level of understanding. It refers to a type of understanding or apprehension such that the individual knows what is being communicated and can make use of the material or idea being communicated without necessarily relating it to other material or seeing its fullest implications.

2.10 Translation

Comprehension as evidenced by the care and accuracy with which the communication is paraphrased or rendered from one language or form of communication to another. Translation is judged on the basis of faithfulness and accuracy; that is, on the extent to which the material in the original communication is preserved although the form of the communication has been altered.

The ability to understand nonliteral statements (metaphor, symbolism, irony, exaggeration).

Skill in translating mathematical verbal material into symbolic statements and vice versa.

2.20 Interpretation

The explanation or summarization of a communication. Whereas translation involves an objective part-for-part rendering of a communication, interpretation involves a reordering, rearrangement, or new view of the material.

The ability to grasp the thought of the work as a whole at any desired level of generality.

The ability to interpret various types of social data.

2.30 Extrapolation

The extension of trends or tendencies beyond the given data to determine implications, consequences, corollaries, effects, etc., which are in accordance with the conditions described in the original communication.

The ability to deal with the conclusions of a work in terms of the immediate inference made from the explicit statements.

Skill in predicting continuation of trends.

3.00 APPLICATION

The use of abstractions in particular and concrete stiuations. The abstractions may be in the form of general ideas, rules of procedures, or generalized methods. The abstractions may also be technical principles, ideas, and theories which must be remembered and applied.

Application to the phenomena discussed in one paper of the scientific terms or concepts used in other papers.

The ability to predict the probable effect of a change in a factor on a biological situation previously at equilibrium.

4.00 ANALYSIS

The breakdown of a communication into its constituent elements or parts such that the relative hierarchy of ideas is made clear and/or the relations between the ideas expressed are made explicit. Such analyses are intended to clarify the communication, to indicate how the communication is organized, and the way in which it manages to convey its effects, as well as its basis and arrangement.

4.10 Analysis of Elements

Identification of the elements included in a communication.

The ability to recognize unstated assumptions.

Skill in distinguishing facts from hypotheses.

4.20 Analysis of Relationships

The connections and interactions between elements and parts of a communication.

Ability to check the consistency of hypotheses with given information and assumptions.

Skill in comprehending the interrelationships among the ideas in a passage.

4.30 Analysis of Organizational Principles

The organization, systematic arrangement, and structure which hold the communication together. This includes the "explicit" as well as "implicit" structure. It includes the bases, necessary arrangement, and mechanics which make the communication a unit.

The ability to recognize form and pattern in literary or artistic works as a means of understanding their meaning.

Ability to recognize the general techniques used in persuasive materials, such as advertising, propaganda, etc.

5.00 SYNTHESIS

The putting together of elements and parts so as to form a whole. This involves the process of working with pieces, parts, elements, etc., and arranging and combining them in such a way as to constitute a pattern or structure not clearly there before.

5.10 Production of a Unique Communication

The development of a communication in which the writer or speaker attempts to convey ideas, feelings, and/or experiences to others.

Skill in writing, using an excellent organization of ideas and statements.

Ability to tell a personal experience effectively.

5.20 Production of a Plan, or Proposed Set of Operations

The development of a plan of work or the proposal of a plan of operations. The plan should satisfy requirements of the task which may be given to the student or which he may develop for himself.

Ability to propose ways of testing hypotheses.

Ability to plan a unit of instruction for a particular teaching situation.

5.30 Derivation of a Set of Abstract Relations

The development of a set of abstract relations either to classify or explain particular data or phenomena, or the deduction of propositions and relations from a set of basic propositions or symbolic representations.

Ability to formulate appropriate hypotheses based upon an analysis of factors involved, and to modify such hypotheses in the light of new factors and considerations.

Ability to make mathematical discoveries and generalizations.

6.00 EVALUATION

Judgments about the value of material and methods for given purposes. Quantitative and qualitative judgments about the extent to which material and methods satisfy criteria. Use of a standard of appraisal. The criteria may be those determined by the student or those which are given to him.

6.10 Judgments in Terms of Internal Evidence

Evaluation of the accuracy of a communication from such evidence as logical accuracy, consistency, and other internal criteria.

Judging by internal standards, the ability to assess general probability of accuracy in reporting facts from the care given to exactness of statement, documentation, proof, etc.

The ability to indicate logical fallacies in arguments.

6.20 Judgments in Terms of External Criteria

Evaluation of material with reference to selected or remembered criteria.

The comparison of major theories, generalizations, and facts about particular cultures.

Judging by external standards, the ability to compare a work with the highest known standards in its field—especially with other works of recognized excellence.

BIBLIOGRAPHY*

ADKINS, DOROTHY C., and KUDER, G. FREDERIC. "The Relation of Primary Mental Abilities to Activity Preference," *Psychometrika, 5* (1940), 251–62.

ADORNO, T. W., *et al. The Authoritarian Personality.* New York: Harper, 1950.

ALLPORT, GORDON W. *The Nature of Prejudice.* Cambridge, Mass.: Addison-Wesley, 1954.

ASCH, SOLOMON E. *Social Psychology.* New York: Prentice-Hall, 1952.

BARKER, ROGER G., DEMBO, T., and LEWIN, K. *Frustration and Regression: An Experiment with Young Children.* Vol. 18, No. 1. Iowa City, Iowa: University of Iowa Studies in Child Welfare, 1941.

BENDER, IRVING. "Changes in Religious Interest—A Retest After Fifteen Years," *Journal of Abnormal and Social Psychology, 57* (1958), 41–46.

BLOOM, BENJAMIN S. "The Thought Processes of Students in Discussion," Chapter I, SIDNEY J. FRENCH (ed.), *Accent on Teaching.* New York: Harper, 1954.

———. *Stability and Change in Human Characteristics.* New York: Wiley, 1964.

———, and BRODER, L. J. *Problem-Solving Processes of College Students.* Chicago: University of Chicago Press, 1950.

BRUNER, JEROME. *The Process of Education.* Cambridge, Mass.: Harvard University Press, 1960.

BUROS, OSCAR K. (ed.). *The Fifth Mental Measurements Yearbook.* Highland Park, N. J.: Gryphon, 1959.

CHAUSOW, HYMEN M. "The Organization of Learning Experiences to Achieve More Effectively the Objectives of Critical Thinking in the General Social Science Course at the Junior College Level." Unpublished Ph.D. dissertation, University of Chicago, 1955.

COLEMAN, JAMES S. *The Adolescent Society.* Glencoe: Free Press, 1961.

DARLEY, JOHN G. "Changes in Measured Attitudes and Adjustments," *Journal of Social Psychology, 9* (1938), 189–99.

DRESSEL, PAUL L. "Interests—Stable or Unstable?" *Journal of Educational Research, 48* (1954), 95–102.

———. *Evaluation in the Basic College at Michigan State University.* New York: Harper, 1958.

———, and MAYHEW, L. B. *General Education: Explorations in Evaluation.* Washington, D.C.: American Council on Education, 1954.

———, and NELSON, CLARENCE H. *Questions and Problems in Science.* Princeton, N.J.: Educational Testing Service, 1956.

DUNKEL, HAROLD B. *General Education in the Humanities.* Washington, D.C.: American Council on Education, 1947.

ENGLISH, HORACE, and ENGLISH, AVA C. *A Comprehensive Dictionary of Psychological and Psychoanalytical Terms.* New York: David McKay, 1958.

ERIKSON, ERIK H. *Childhood and Society.* New York: Norton, 1950.

FESTINGER, LEON. *A Theory of Cognitive Dissonance.* Evanston, Ill.: Row, Peterson, 1957.

*Excluding test sources cited in Part II.

———, and CARLSMITH, JAMES M. "Cognitive Consequences of Forced Compliance," *Journal of Abnormal and Social Psychology, 58* (1959), 203–10.

FROMM, ERICH. *Escape from Freedom.* New York: Rinehart, 1941.

FURST, EDWARD J. *Constructing Evaluation Instruments.* New York: David McKay, 1958.

GARDNER, JOHN W. *Excellence.* New York: Harper, 1961.

GOOD, CARTER V. *Dictionary of Education* (2d ed.). New York: McGraw Hill, 1959.

Harvard University Committee on the Objectives of a General Education in a Free Society. *General Education in a Free Society.* Cambridge, Mass.: Harvard University Press, 1945.

HEIDER, FRITZ. *The Psychology of Inter-Personal Relations.* New York: Wiley, 1958.

JACOB, PHILLIP E. *Changing Values in College.* New York: Harper, 1957.

JAHODA, MARIE. "Psychological Issues in Civil Liberties," *American Psychologist, 11* (1956), 234–40.

JAMES, WILLIAM. *The Principles of Psychology.* Vol. I. New York: Holt, 1890.

JOHNSON, DONALD M. *The Psychology of Thought and Judgment.* New York: Harper, 1955.

KELLY, E. LOWELL. "Consistency of the Adult Personality," *American Psychology, 10* (1955), 659–81.

KELMAN, HERBERT C. "Compliance, Identification, and Internalization, Three Processes of Attitude Change." *Journal of Conflict Resolution, 2* (1958), 51–60.

LEWIN, KURT. "Group Decision and Social Change," in THEODORE M. NEWCOMB, and EUGENE L. HARTLEY (eds.), *Readings in Social Psychology.* New York: Holt, 1947.

MCKEACHIE, WILBERT J. "Procedures and Techniques of Teaching: A Survey of Experimental Studies," Chapter 8 in NEVITT SANFORD, (ed.), *The American College.* New York: Wiley, 1962.

MASLOW, ABRAHAM H. "Cognition of Being in the Peak Experiences," *Journal of Genetic Psychology, 94* (1959), 43–66.

MAYER, MARTIN. *The Schools.* New York: Harper, 1961.

MAYHEW, LEWIS B. "And in Attitudes," Chapter 4 in PAUL L. DRESSEL (ed.), *Evaluation in the Basic College at Michigan State University.* New York: Harper, 1958.

MORRIS, G. C. *Educational Objectives of Higher Secondary School Science.* Melbourne, Australia: Australian Council on Educational Research, 1961.

MORRISON, J. CAYCE. *The Puerto Rican Study, 1953–1957.* New York: Board of Education, 1958.

NELSON, ERLAND N. P. "Persistence of Attitudes of College Students Fourteen Years Later," *Psychological Monographs,* No. 373, 1954.

NEWCOMB, THEODORE M. *Personality and Social Change.* New York: Dryden Press, 1943.

PACE, C. ROBERT, and STERN, GEORGE G. "An Approach to the Measurement of Psychological Characteristics of College Environments," *Journal of Educational Psychology, 49* (1958), 269–77.

PECK, ROBERT F., and HAVIGHURST, ROBERT J. *The Psychology of Character Development.* New York: Wiley, 1960.

PITTS, JESSE R. "Introduction" in TALCOTT, PARSONS, *et al.* (eds.), *Theories of Society, Volume II.* New York: Free Press of *Glencoe, 1961.*

PLANT, WALTER T. "Changes in Ethnocentrism Associated with a Four Year College Education," *Journal of Educational Psychology, 49* (1958), 162–65.

RHINE, RAYMOND J. "A Concept Formation Approach to Attitude Acquisition," *Psychological Review, 65* (1958), 362–70.

RIESMAN, DAVID. *The Lonely Crowd.* New Haven, Conn.: Yale University Press, 1961

ROKEACH, MILTON. *The Open and Closed Mind.* New York: Basic Books, 1960.

ROSENBERG, MILTON J. "Cognitive Structure and Attitudinal Affect," *Journal of Abnormal and Social Psychology, 53* (1956), 637–72.

RUSSELL, DAVID H. *Children's Thinking.* Boston: Ginn, 1956.

SANFORD, NEVITT. "Personality Development During the College Years," *Journal of Social Issues, 12* (1956), 3–70.

SAWIN, ENOCH I., and LOREE, M. RAY. "Broadening the Base in Evaluation," *School Review, 67* (1959), 79–92.

SCHEERER, MARTIN. "Cognitive Theory," Chapter 3 in *Handbook of Social Psychology,* Volume I. Cambridge, Mass.: Addison-Wesley, 1954.

SCHEFFLER, ISRAEL. *The Language of Education.* Springfield, Ill.: Charles C. Thomas, 1960.

STERN, GEORGE C., STEIN, MORRIS I., and BLOOM, BENJAMIN S. *Methods in Personality Assessment.* Glencoe, Ill.: Free Press of Glencoe, 1956.

STRONG, E. K., JR. *Vocational Interests Eighteen Years After College.* Minneapolis: University of Minnesota Press, 1955.

SUCHMAN, J. RICHARD. *The Elementary School Training Program in Scientific Inquiry.* Title VII, Project Number 216, National Defense Education Act of 1958. Grant No. 7-11-038. Urbana, Ill.: University of Illinois, 1962.

SUPER, DONALD E., and OVERSTREET, P. L. *The Vocational Maturity of Ninth-Grade Boys.* New York: Teachers College, Columbia University, Bureau of Publications, 1960.

THISTLETHWAITE, DONALD. "Attitudes and Structure as Factors in the Distortion of Reasoning." *Journal of Abnormal and Social Psychology, 45* (1950), 442–58.

TOWLE, CHARLOTTE. *Learning in Education for the Professions, as Seen in Education for Social Work.* Chicago: University of Chicago Press, 1954.

TYLER, RALPH W. *Constructing Achievement Tests.* Columbus, Ohio: Ohio State University Press, 1934.

———. "The Functions of Measurement in Improving Instruction," Chapter 2 in E. F. LINDQUIST (ed.), *Educational Measurement.* Washington, D.C.: American Council on Education, 1951.

VERNON, PHILIP E. *Personality Tests and Assessments.* London: Methuen and Co., Ltd., 1953.

WEBSTER, HAROLD. "Changes in Attitudes During College," *Journal of Educational Psychology, 49* (1958), 109–17.

WERTHEIMER, MAX. *Productive Thinking.* New York: Harper, 1954.

WHITE, ROBERT. "Motivation Reconsidered—The Concept of Competence," *Psychological Review, 66* (1959), 297–333.

WOODRUFF, ASAHEL. *A Study of the Directive Factors in Individual Behavior.* Ph.D. thesis. Chicago: University of Chicago, 1941.